The Town of Warwick in 1903

Source: *Mueller's Atlas of Orange County*

Days Gone By

A History in Pictures
Town of Warwick, New York
1827-1945

Centennial Celebration Edition
The Historical Society of the Town of Warwick
1906-2006

Compiled by
Sue Gardner
Gary Randall
Kathy Randall

PUBLISHING
Warwick, New York
www.KeeneBooks.com

Days Gone By

A History in Pictures Town of Warwick, New York 1827-1945

Copyright © 2006 Historical Society of the Town of Warwick

Published by Keene Publishing Warwick, NY

ISBN-10: 0-9766805-0-5
ISBN-13: 978-0-9766805-0-5

All rights reserved. No part of this book may be used or reproduced in any manner whatsoever without written permission except in the case of brief quotations embodied in published articles and reviews where full credit to book title, the Historical Society of the Town of Warwick, NY, and compilation editors is provided. Please send copy of published article to Keene Publishing PO Box 54 Warwick, NY 10990. For information, contact Keene Publishing at the address above, via email info@keenebooks.com, or see our Web site at www.KeeneBooks.com.

Quantity Purchases

Companies, professional groups, nonprofits, and other organizations may qualify for special discounts when ordering quantities of this title. For information, write Special Sales, Keene Publishing, PO Box 54 Warwick, NY 10990, call 845-987-7750 or email to info@KeeneBooks.com.

Historical Society of the Town of Warwick

For more information on the Historical Society of the Town of Warwick, visit their Web site at www.warwickhistoricalsociety.org, email info@warwickhistoricalsociety.org, or call 845-986-3236.

Publisher's Cataloging-in-Publication Data

Historical Society of the Town of Warwick.

Days Gone By: A History in Pictures, Town of Warwick, New York, 1827-1945
/ Compiled by Sue Gardner, Gary Randall and Kathy Randall
—Centennial celebration ed.—Warwick, N.Y.: Keene Publishing 2006.

ill. p. (256) cm. Includes index.

ISBN 0-9766805-0-5

1. Warwick (NY)—History—Pictorial works. 2. Warwick (NY)—Buildings, structures, etc.—Pictorial works. 3. Orange County (NY)—History—Pictorial works.

I. Historical Society of the Town of Warwick. II. Gardner, Sue. III. Randall, Gary. IV. Randall, Kathy. V. Title

F129. H5   2006   2006921889   974.731 His

Printed in the United States of America.

10 9 8 7 6 5 4 3 2 1

Dedication

A century ago, on April 19 of 1906, a public meeting was held at the YMCA building in Warwick (today this is known as the 1810 House museum) to organize a historical society. The founders of our group intended that the organization would encourage study about and preservation of the history of the Town of Warwick.

We began by collecting documents, books, and photographs, by noting and marking historic sites, and by doing research and presenting our findings to the community. In 1916 we acquired the Shingle House as a museum, and since that time with the help and encouragement of Mr. and Mrs. Madison Lewis and the hard work and generosity of many members of the community, we have gradually built a collection of artifacts and historic buildings that is one of the most significant in the State of New York.

A century later, the Historical Society of the Town of Warwick now owns and maintains the Old School Baptist Meeting House, Lewis Park, the 1810 House, Baird's Tavern, the Hasbrouck Carriage House, the Shingle House, the Sly Barn, the Azariah Ketchum House, and the Old School Baptist Cemetery. Our members, volunteers, and officers work hard throughout the year to keep our seven buildings, properties, and collection preserved for the future; we could not do it without the continual support of our community.

This book is dedicated to all those hard workers and generous donors who over the past 100 years have contributed in so many ways to the preservation of Warwick's historic heritage.

Acknowledgments and Disclaimer

We would like to extend our deepest gratitude to Sue Gardner whose tireless efforts pulled this book together and to Gary and Kathy Randall who assisted Sue from concept to final product.

Special thanks also go to the Albert Wisner Public Library. Six years ago the library and the Society began a cooperative project to gather, properly house, and catalog our historical papers and photographs. This book is one of the projects made possible because of that support.

The compilation authors and the board members would like to thank everyone who has shared his or her photos with us for this special publication, and over our 100 years. Old methods of record keeping have left some gaps in knowing the names of donors of some items to our collection; our apologies in advance if we have missed a few. Please let us know if we've shown your donated photo and have not properly attributed it.

Ordering Photo Reprints

Reprints of many of the photos are available; you can visit us on the Web at www.warwickhistoricalsociety.org or call (845) 986-3236 to find out more. We cannot reproduce photos that are in private collections, however, without permission of the owners.

Table of Contents

Introduction	7
Early Portraits	13
Amity	23
Bellvale	29
Edenville	35
Florida Village	43
Greenwood Lake	57
Lake (Lawton)	67
Little York	71
New Milford	75
Pine Island	81
Warwick Village	87
Warwick Town (other areas)	103
Wisner (Stone Bridge)	113
Business and Industry	117
Celebrations and Events	143
Daily Life	165
Education and Health	185
Hospitality and Tourism	201
Houses of Worship	153
Organizations	211
Railroads	219
Sports	235
Notes	243
Index	246

Days Gone By   A History in Pictures Town of Warwick, New York 1827-1945

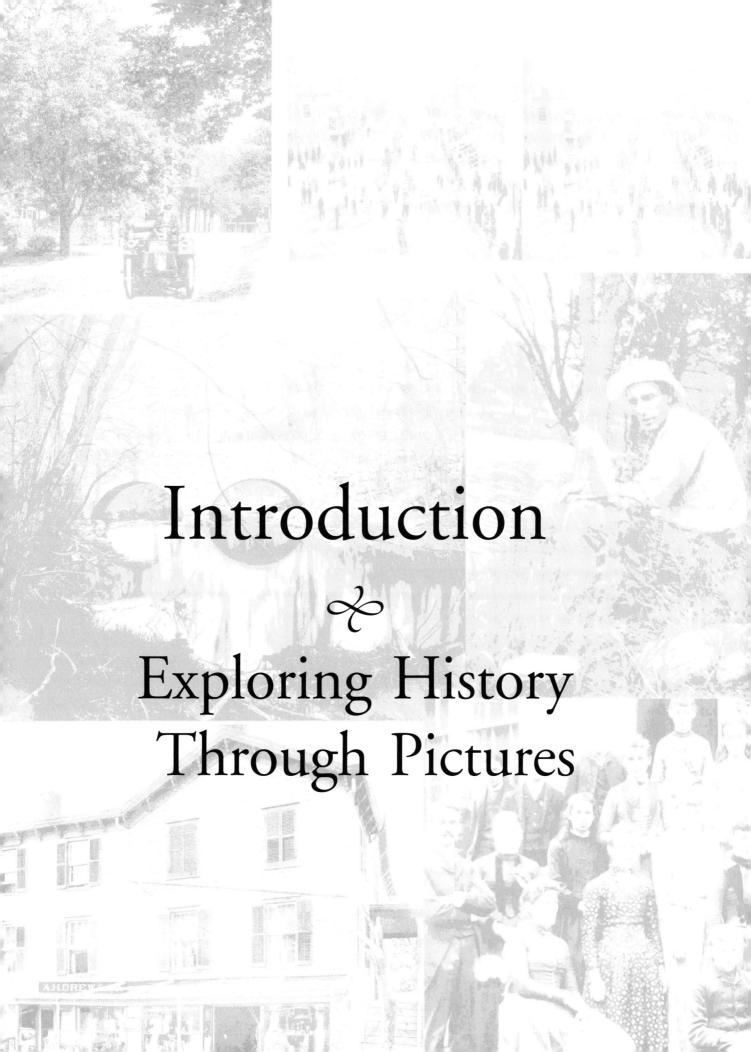

Introduction
&
Exploring History Through Pictures

Exploring History Through Pictures

Pictures are a mirror of ourselves as a community: our struggles, our successes and failures, and our daily lives. Looking at them makes us stronger human beings by helping us recognize that our strength lies in our common experiences—the bonds that pull us together and not apart. Our historic heritage is one of those connections.

The people who dwelled here before us did the best they could with the resources and tools at hand even as we do now. Enjoy these glimpses into the past and reflect on the love for Warwick that they give witness to—that reaches forward to encourage our citizens today.

Arrangement of the Book

The layout of this book is intended to both celebrate our historic hamlets and highlight various aspects of our entire town as a community. This may present some challenge for those who wish to locate the photos of a particular area; but as with all things historical, half of the fun of research is turning up little surprises you weren't expecting along the way. There is an index at the end to help you find pictures by hamlet or by subject.

A Word About the Dates

Many of the dates assigned to our photos are approximate; we have done the best we can, taking into account the format of postcards where possible, the type of photographic print, and physical clues in the picture. The "c." in front of the date is an abbreviation for circa and as such represents our best estimate of the date. Actual dates could be within a few decades, in some cases.

Warwick's Early Photographers

This book could not exist without the people who took the time to record our history in images. Some were professional photographers; many were ordinary citizens. Our research into the professional photographers continues, but at this time we know some of the names and dates associated with them:

Name	Year(s)	Studio Location
Arnold, Frank L.	by 1899+	*Advertiser* Block
Elston, Roy	1930's-1940s	Warwick
Morely, J. F.	1884+	Warwick, corner of West
Razey, James	c. 1870-	Chester & Florida
Still, Edwin F.	by 1866+	Warwick, corner of West
Thomas, William C.	c.1870s	Warwick
Welles, Frank J.	1882+	Greenwood Lake
Williams, Gilbert A.	1931+	Maple Ave., Warwick

The Historical Society of the Town of Warwick

Photographic Rooms
c. 1870-1880
Collection of Florence Tate

Early photographic studio at Corner of West and Main in the Village of Warwick.[1] This photo is from a stereoscope and shows skylight and picture windows for natural light on the top floor of the West Street side. Offices of the *Warwick Advertiser*, founded in 1866, are on the left side.

The Joslyn Collection

In 2004, Duane Joslyn donated to the Society a large collection of glass plate negatives from the studio shown above. His father had moved into the studio and many of the negatives were still there. We assume from the subject matter that they are primarily the work of E. F. Still.

Buttonwood
c. 1900
Reprinted from Florida Historical book[2]

Buttonwood, home of photographer James Razey (1851-?) 400 Route 17A. James purchased Broadview Farm, and built the unique Razey Cottage in Chester. He later occupied Buttonwood Farm on the Florida-Goshen border.

9

Dating Postcards by Format

Pioneer Era (1893-1898)
Although there were earlier scattered issues, most pioneer cards in today's collections begin with the cards placed on sale at the Columbian Exposition in Chicago, Illinois, on May 1, 1893. These were illustrations on government printed postal cards and on privately printed souvenir cards. The government postal card had the imprinted 1-cent stamp while the souvenir cards required a 2-cent adhesive postage stamp to be applied to it. Writing was not permitted on the address side of the card.

Private Mailing Card Era (1898-1901)
On May 19, 1898, private printers were granted permission, by an act of Congress, to print and sell cards that bore the inscription "Private Mailing Card." Today we call these cards "PMCs." Postage required was now a 1-cent adhesive stamp. A dozen or more American printers began to take postcards seriously. Writing was still not permitted on the address side; however, many publishers often left a wider border on the side or bottom of the view side so a short message could be added.

Postcard Era (1901-1907)
The use of the word "Postcard" was granted by the government to private printers on December 4, 1901. In this era, private citizens began to take black-and-white photographs and have them printed on paper with postcard backs. Writing was still not permitted on the address side.

Undivided Back Era (1893-1907)
The above three eras can also be grouped into the general heading of "undivided back."

Divided Back Era (1907-1914)
Postcards with a divided back, that is, with a printed vertical line down the middle, were permitted starting March 1, 1907 (the address to be written on the right side and written messages to be on the left). Many millions of cards were published during this period. Up to this point most cards were printed in Germany, which was far ahead of this country in the lithographic processes. With the advent of World War I, the supply of postcards had to come from England to the United States.

White Border Era (1915-1930)
Most of our postcards were printed in the USA during this period. To save ink, a border was left around the view; thus we classify them as "White Border Cards." High cost of labor, inexperience, and public taste caused production of poor quality cards. High competition in a narrowing market caused many publishers to go out of business.

Linen Era (1930-1944)
New printing processes allowed printing on postcards with a high rag content that caused a "linen-like" finish. These cheap cards allowed the use of gaudy dyes for coloring. The firm of Curt Teich flourished with their line of linen postcards. Many important events in history were recorded on these cards.

Photochrome Era (1945 to present)
The "chrome" postcards started to dominate the scene soon after they were launched by the Union Oil Company in their western service stations in 1939. Mike Roberts pioneered with his "WESCO" cards soon after World War II. Three-dimensional postcards also appeared in this era.

Dating Postcards by Physical Clues

In addition to the postcard format dates (see chart below), you can sometimes determine dates by physical clues in the photo. For example, for the business section of the Village of Warwick some clues are:

Physical Clue	Date Range
Methodist Church Steeple (Clocktower bldg.)/Main St.	Before 1918 (steeple was destroyed)
Electric/phone lines/Main St.	After Feb. 19, 1898
Fire hydrants/Main St.	After 1872
Railroad station/South St. & Railroad Ave.	Wooden: between 1862 & 1893 Stone: after 1893
Near corner Main near corner of South St.	Wooden store block: before 1879 Brick store block: after 1879
Demerest Hotel/South St. & Railroad Ave.	Wooden: 1865-1887 Brick: after 1887 Demerest Hall attached: after 1872
Red Swan Inn/Oakland Ave.	After 1902
Village Hall (in old Reformed Church)/Main St.	After 1890

Preserving Today's Pictures for Tomorrow

As the history of our Town continues to unfold, we must remember to do our part to record and preserve that history for future generations. Technology constantly changes, and, along with giving us new tools for recording our families and community, it presents new challenges. The digital photos of today will probably not be readable within a few decades; prints from our own computer printers instead of from a traditional photo process will fade much more quickly. Here are a few tips to help ensure that your photos will be helping people connect to our past 100 years or more from now:

1. Send your best digital photos to a photo processing facility for printing. Do this regularly, perhaps as part of your annual holiday preparations or New Year's resolutions.
2. If you choose to print everything at home, get a special "archival ink" cartridge for your printer and use acid-free paper for your best shots. They are worth it!
3. Do not store photos in albums that have a "self adhesive" surface. These adhesives eventually damage the photo.
4. Buy acid-free photo albums or boxes.
5. Store your photos in a cool, dry place out of the light.
6. Buy a special photo marking pen to write on the back of the photos. Everyday pens and markers can eventually bleed through and damage the image.
7. Make sure you DO label the subject and the date! Even close relatives may not be able to guess who is shown or where they were taken.
8. If you have a great shot of contemporary events or places in Town, consider donating a copy to the Historical Society archive now—someone cleaning out your possessions years from now will probably throw most of them away!

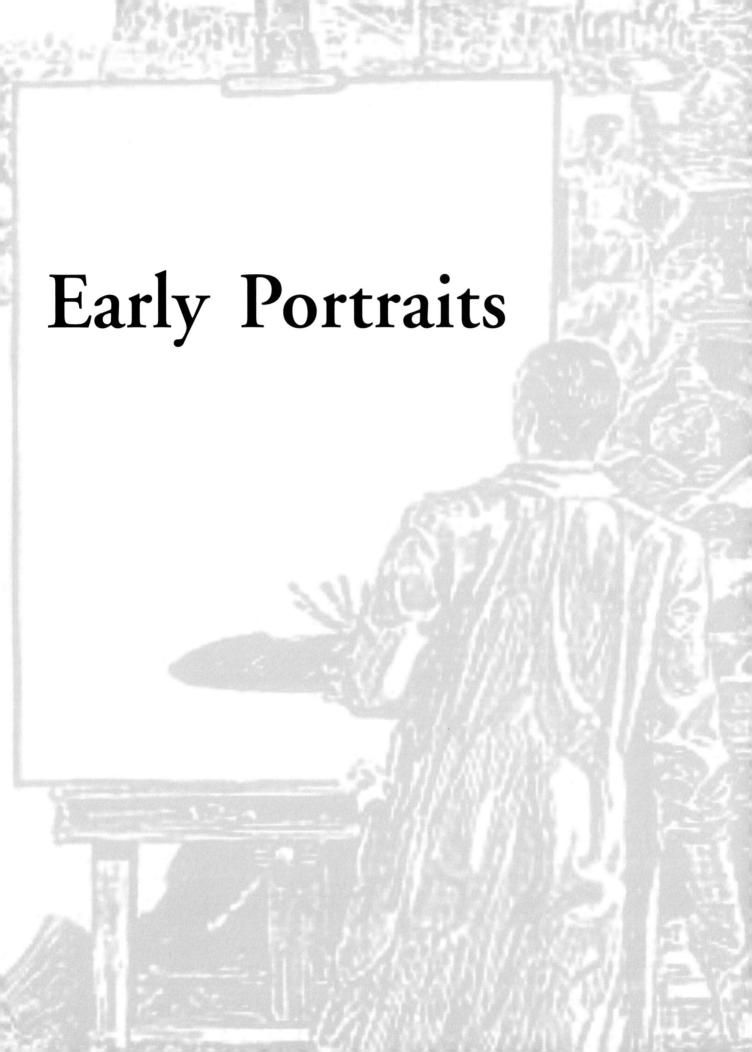

Early Portraits

Early Portrait Artists in Warwick

The earliest images that we have of life in Warwick are painted portraits. They tell us not only what some of our citizens of the early 1800s looked and dressed like, but also something about their daily life and occupations. Their clothes are generally simple or even austere, in keeping with the sentiment of the times that imitation of elaborate English or European modes of dress indicated a sympathy with monarchies that still posed a threat to the new nation. There were no art academies here, and many artists traveled to England and Europe to study. Yet while portraits of European aristocrats during this period were usually highly stylized and idealized, artists in America struggled to accurately replicate bone structure and proportions, which they thought revealed a person's inner character. Usually the subject was painted with a prop or background that indicated the subject's career, business, or personal interests.

Warwick citizens could draw on the talents of New York City artists as well as itinerant painters who traveled the Hudson Valley. We were fortunate to also have local portrait artists of our own.

Elias Coe 1794?-1843

Elias Van Arsdale Coe was a physician who practiced locally, as seen in a description of an operation he performed in *Under Old Rooftrees* (p. 157).[3] It seems logical that someone trained to be a keen observer of physical symptoms might also apply this skill to his paintings. Two of his portraits are included in the National Gallery of Art (www.nga.gov):

Henry W. Houston

The portrait of Henry W. Houston (National Portrait Gallery Catalog no. 1957.11.6) was painted in 1837. Henry was born in 1797 and died on Nov. 28, 1869, according to his tombstone at the Edenville Church cemetery. We can surmise from the compass and slide rule that he holds in the portrait that he was a surveyor.

Phebe Houston

Mrs. Phebe Houston (National Portrait Gallery Catalog no. 1953.5.6) was painted in 1837. The wife of Henry W. Houston, Phebe Dusinberre Houston was born in 1799 and died on Feb. 12, 1871, according to her tombstone at the Edenville Church cemetery. She was the daughter of Daniel Coe Dusinberre.

Milton McConnell 1820-?

Milton McConnell was a recently identified painter of local portraits; we know little about him at this time. He painted local Wisner family members in the mid 1800s. He was the son of John and Ann McConnell, baptized at the Amity Presbyterian Church on Sept. 13, 1820. He was a thirty-year-old in the household on the 1850 Census for Warwick, and apparently was unmarried in 1850. His occupation in 1850 is "limner," another term for portrait artist. He and a relative, "Linen," were called out of NYC to paint the Wisner portraits, according to a family story. By 1857 he had married and relocated to New Jersey, where his eldest daughter was born, as stated on the 1880 Census for Caldwell, NJ.

Colonel John Hathorn
c. 1850-1880
by C. Brown, Jr.
Cabinet card from the collection of Nancy Gifford.

This composite portrait is the only image of one of Warwick's first leaders, Colonel John Hathorn (1749-1825).[4] The painting itself has been lost, and we only have a "cabinet card" photograph of it provided by one of his descendants. The portrait was commissioned by Rev. Ezra Sanford (1793-1883), who owned the Hathorn house. The painting was done long after he died using descriptions of him provided by his descendants, and by examining their own facial structure and appearance. According to one of Hathorn's grandsons, "he was about 5 feet 7 inches, of medium size, rather slender, fair complexion, brown hair and very bright keen gray eyes, of an easy amiable disposition, genial, impulsive, and very energetic" (from a letter by James B. Hathorn to Lyman Draper, Oct. 29, 1877). He was the leader of the local militia during the Revolutionary War, and one of the commanding officers at the tragedy of the Battle of Minisink. His house still stands on Hathorn Road.

William Henry Seward
c. 1910
by C. Brower Darst
Historical Society of the Town of Warwick

This portrait of William Henry Seward by C. Brower Darst hangs in the S.S. Seward Institute and is on permanent loan to the Florida Union Free School District from the Historical Society of the Town of Warwick.

William Henry Seward (1801-1872) was the third son of Samuel Sweezy Seward, who was destined to leave the tiny hamlet of Florida, his birthplace, and go on to fame and a certain degree of fortune. His fond recollections of the Seward slaves who, while always treated with respect and lived in the warm family kitchen and attic, first made him aware of the gross injustice inherent in the slave system. He attended Union College, studying law, and graduated in 1820 with high honors. He became anti-slavery, which meant he opposed the expansion of slavery and was pro free soil, after observing the conditions of slavery while working in Georgia. He then read law in Florida, New York and Goshen, and joined his practice with his father-in-law, Judge Elijah Miller, in Auburn, New York. He served as State Senator from 1831-1834, and then was elected Governor of New York from 1839-1843. After his second term as Governor, he assisted his father in establishing S.S. Seward Institute in Florida. He then became a U.S. Senator (1849-1861) and was Secretary of State under presidents Abraham Lincoln and Andrew Johnson (1861-1869). He survived an assasination attempt on the same night Lincoln was shot. He was instrumental in the purchase of Alaska, for which he was at first ridiculed. Alaska celebrates "Seward Day" in March.

Seward Monument
c. 1930
Reprinted from Florida Historical book [2]

The Seward Monument on North Main Street that honors William Henry Seward was sculpted by the renowned Daniel Chester French and still looks directly across the street at the Seward Mansion (today the Professional Building); behind him is the still vibrant "Institute" founded by his father. The monument is listed on the National Register of Historic Places.

Emancipation Proclamation
c. 1863
Reprinted from Florida Historical book [2]

"First reading of the Emancipation Proclamation," an engraving based on the painting by Francis Carpenter. William Henry Seward is in the front, wearing white pants.

Formal Engraving with Signature
c. 1840
Reprinted from Florida Historical book [2]

Formal engraving of William Henry Seward with his signature below.

Seward was honored with having his portrait on the 1891 $50 Treasury Note. These are so rare now that in 2005 one such note sold for nearly $300,000!

These portraits, painted by different artists two years apart, were intended to hang side by side. We can guess this from the matching tree and background detail that was included.

Mary Burt Jones
1829
Painted by Elias Van Arsdale Coe
Courtesy Private Collection

Mary Burt Jones was the favorite daughter of Warwick's James Burt, a New York State Senator. She and Nathaniel were married in 1811. A transcription of her husband's memoirs in the collection of the Historical Society of the Town of Warwick gives many details of their life together.

Nathaniel Jones
1827
Painted by Frederick R. Spencer
Courtesy Private Collection

Nathaniel Jones (1788-1866) came to Warwick from Rhode Island in May 1808 to teach school, and later became a businessman and then a politician. He served in the New York State Assembly and later the U. S. Congress from 1837-1841.

Jones Homestead
date unknown
Courtesy of Richard Hull

This house which stood at the corner of Church and Main (looking from Lewis Park) appears to have been the structure that was built and occupied by the Joneses as their home and store, known at one time as the "Barker House" after later residents. Hylah Hasbrouck describes this house in her history of Fountain Square. It housed the first post office and a store run by John McKee, and then Milton and Thomas McEwen (McKewn). Demolished in recent decades, there is now a parking lot where it once stood.

Dr. James P. Young
1831
Painted by Elias Van Arsdale Coe
Collection of James Cline and Victor Robinson

Dr. James P. Young (1791-1835) was an avid mineralogist as well as a physician. His stone home still stands at the corner of Pine Island Turnpike and Edenville Rd. He lived on one of Warwick's early main roads, and he treated notables such as Aaron Burr.[5] He and Dr. Heron drew a map of Warwick's geology in 1831. The artist alludes to Young's favorite hobby by showing him holding some of his prized specimens. He apparently also was involved with an unknown water project, as seen by the spillway or dam shown in the background.

Justus Dill
c. 1860
Artist Unknown
Historical Society of the Town of Warwick

This portrait of Justus Dill (1804-1887), once hung in the Dill House, now hangs in Baird Tavern museum in Warwick. He stands in front of the building which still retains his name, on Main Street, Florida. Justus Dill, born on September 24, 1804, and his wife, the former Emily Mapes, settled in Florida and started a family. By 1831 the thriving Dill Carriage Shop stood almost directly across from the future site of the Dill House. The Dill brothers, Justus and William, thought this would be a prime location for a business that could meet various needs of travelers on the busy highway through the village. Florida's preeminent entrepreneur planned a three-story building with a restaurant, hotel rooms, meeting rooms, and a ballroom. At the top a carved stone would proclaim "DILL HOUSE." In 1850, Justus Dill sold the building and it continued to be run as a hotel. Justus died July 8, 1887.

Henry William Herbert
After 1926
From an earlier portrait by R. L. Boyer
Historical Society of the Town of Warwick

This portrait of Henry William Herbert (1807-1858) is from an earlier work by R. L. Boyer for Derrydale Press. Writing under the pseudonym "Frank Forester," Herbert was a prolific writer of sporting tales. He was born in England of a noble family and was sent to America to live in 1831, apparently in punishment for some indiscretion. He lived in Newark, New Jersey, at his home The Cedars. Warwick was one of his favorite haunts and he wrote many pieces about hunting and fishing here, including the book, *Warwick Woodlands*.[6] As an avid sportsman, in his later writings he deplored the decline of the environment and the wildlife that he so loved to hunt, and so was one of the first proponents of conservation.

Thomas Ward
Before 1857
by (Henry?) Van Ingen
Historical Society of the Town of Warwick

The Wawayanda House, where author Henry W. Herbert stayed, was run by his friend Tom Ward (?-1857). Called in his works "Tom Draw," many anecdotes in his book *Warwick Woodlands* tell of this oversized, genial innkeeper of the mid 1800s. In his memorial essay when Ward died, Herbert describes him as "the frankest, most jovial, wittiest and best hearted of companions…an innocent eccentric…his circumference some 2 or 3 inches greater than his height of 5'6"…not only one of the most powerful but one of the most enduring and fleet-footed men I have ever met with…there was a look of the readiest and clearest intelligence in his bright masking eyes which speedily betrayed to the observer a mind of extraordinary quickness, sagacity, humor, and imagination…"[7] Henry Van Ingen was the first professor of art at Vassar, and we conjecture that the "Van Ingen" of this portrait was he.

Jasper Francis Cropsey
c. 1850
by Edward L. Mooney
Collection of the Newington-Cropsey Foundation

This portrait of Jasper Francis Cropsey (1823-1900) was painted by Edward L. Mooney. Born on Staten Island, as a young man Cropsey pursued his artistic talents and joined the ranks of the Hudson River School of painters. He traveled here in the 1840s and painted Greenwood Lake. He met West Milford resident Maria Cooley, whom he married. After traveling in Europe they built an elaborate mansion, Aladdin, here in Warwick in 1866. They lived at Aladdin until 1884, when debt forced them to sell the house. They relocated to Hastings-on-Hudson. Cropsey paintings of Warwick are beautiful images of the idealized pastoral beauty of the Warwick Valley.[8]

Aladdin (Barr Castle)
c. 1915
Historical Society of the Town of Warwick

Jasper and Maria Cropsey's mansion, which they named *Aladdin,* was magnificent. It stood on Moe Mountain, its entrance nearly opposite the intersection of Warwick Turnpike and Black Rock Road. Roger Kling later owned the property and named it *Barr Castle*. It changed hands several times, and sadly burned down on Sept. 23, 1909, in a spectacular blaze that could be seen all over the valley. All that remains is an historical marker and a foundation on private lands. You can still experience the view that they had, and which Cropsey painted, from the drive of the Warwick Conference Center.

"A Cabin on Greenwood Lake" painted by J. F. Cropsey in 1879. Maria Cooley Cropsey was the daughter of Isaac P. Cooley. Their homestead was on Belcher's Creek, near Greenwood Lake.

Unknown source

Samuel Sweezy Seward
c. 1810
Artist Unknown
Reprinted from Florida Historical book [2]

Samuel Sweezy Seward was born in 1768 and lived until 1849. In lieu of monetary share in his father's estate, Samuel received an education in the field of medicine. In 1795 he and his wife moved to the tiny hamlet of Florida where he started a medical practice, and soon became the first vice-president of the Orange County Medical Society. He was an elected member of the New York State Legislature, a county judge, and then the first judge of the Court of Common Pleas. He also ventured into the mercantile business, became a shrewd financier, kept a farm and owned a fleet of schooners to ship local produce from Newburgh to New York City. The schooners brought back sugar and molasses on their return trips.

Today, he is best remembered in Florida for his interest in education. He was one of the first school commissioners of the Washington Academy, and at the age of eighty he established his own "Institute" of higher learning, S.S. Seward Institute.

Amity

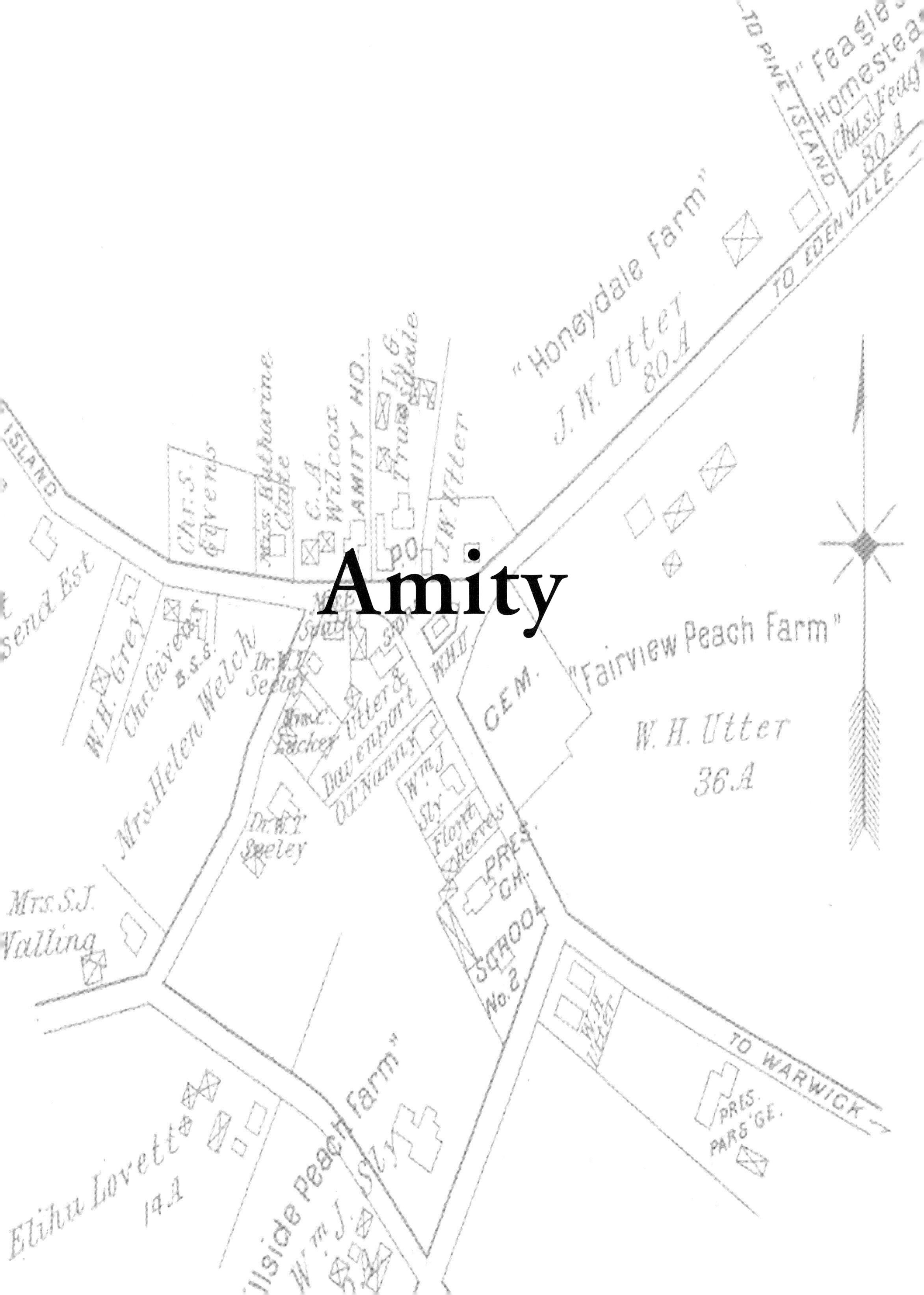

"Feagles Homestead" Chas. Feagle 80 A

TO EDENVILLE

TO PINE ISLAND

"Honeydale Farm" J. W. Utter 80 A

L. G. Truesdale

J. W. Utter

AMITY HO.

P.O.

C. A. Wilcox

Miss Katharine Clark

Chr. S. Givens

TO PINE ISLAND

Sena Est

W. H. Grey

Chr. Givens

B. S. S.

Mrs. Helen Welch

Dr. W. T. Seeley

Smith

Mrs. C. Tucker

Utter & Davenport

O. T. Nanny

W. H. D.

"Fairview Peach Farm" W. H. Utter 36 A

CEM.

Wm. J. Sly

Floyd Reeves

PRES. CH.

SCHOOL No. 2

Dr. W. T. Seeley

Mrs. S. J. Walling

Elihu Lovett 14 A

"Hillside Peach Farm"

Wm. J. Sly

W. H. Utter

PRES. PARS'GE

TO WARWICK

Amity

The name "Amity" is from the French "amitie," or friendship. The area was known as "Pochuck" for its proximity to the Pochuck Creek in early times. Pochuck is derived from a Native American name meaning "out of the way place." This name was used in legal documents by the 1720s, and at least to 1776, as shown on Erskine's maps. Around 1796 when the Amity Presbyterian Church was founded, the name changed to Amity. That name is recorded by 1829, as seen on David H. Burr's map of Orange and Rockland.

One of its earliest settlers was Thomas Ferrier (b. 1705) who came here from Connecticut. Other colonials to settle in Amity included Charles Knapp, a Revolutionary War veteran under John Hathorn, and Seely Sayre. An extract from the diary of Sylvanus Seely in 1786 mentions the little community:

28 Sep. This morning set off for Pochuck at 9 am and heard that Daddy was gone to Seely Sayre's. This place is on the side of the Drowned Lands and has a fine prospect of them. I have come near to ten miles from where I lodged. Seely Sayre took his horses and he went with me in pursuit of my Father…

In 1859 the following businesses are listed in a state-wide directory by Adams, Sampson & Co: Horace G. Sayer, Blacksmith; Edsall Ferrier, Clergy; I. Hoyt, Country Store; Robert Ferrier and Daniel Nanny, Distillers of Spirits; H. G. Sayer, Hotel; and Henry C. Seely, physician.

A description of Amity in Victorian times is found in an essay by a schoolgirl in 1883:

My native village consists of about one hundred and thirty inhabitants and does not increase much in size on account of there being no manufacturers and railroads. It has a school house, post office, church, cemetery, hotel, public hall, two stores, two creameries, a shoemaker, a wagonmaker's shop, blacksmith and harness, one clergyman, two physicians, two painters, one carpenter, several farm laborers. It is situated upon a hill and has beautiful surrounding sceneries.

The community's life revolved around the church. It was a sort of community center; Professor Sweezy conducted singing classes there in the winter, and plays and concerts took place there, as well as dances.

The general store was run by the Trusdell family. Lewis Layton ran the store before this (c. 1870), and it was home to the Langlitz family in 1950. Miss Mabel Trusdell, whose father was the last to operate the store, remembered that the second story of that building was a dance hall, and many dances were held to the tunes of Dayton & Tannery's Orchestra. There was an Amity Cornet Band, and they held concerts on Tuesday nights in a bandstand on the corner.

That Amity's early citizens did not lack for culture and sophistication is further attested to by the fact that in just one family, that of John McConnell, one of his sons—Milton McConnell (b. 1820)—was a "limner" (portrait painter) in the early 1800s, and did portraits of local families including the Wisners. Another relative, Norman McConnell, was a physician who graduated from the University of New York. A list of some of the professional men of Amity is included in a book by Carrie Timlow Feagles about the Amity Presbyterian Church.[9]

While Amity lacked a large community, it is nonetheless a famous locale, for it is in the heart of the Franklin Marble deposit and was, and continues to be, a destination for geologists and rock hunters. Books that document the many minerals—some rare—go back to the early 1800s. The Amity area has the distinction of being the "type locality," or place of first discovery and naming, of several minerals including Warwickite, Clintonite, and Edenite.

Amity Main Street
1915
Collection of Barbra Morgiewicz

The main street in Amity as seen from Newport Bridge Road looking from the store and hotel toward cemetery. Cupola of church steeple shown at right was destroyed by a storm in the 1920s.

Trusdell General Store
Amity Hotel on left.
c. 1875-1902
Collection of Valerie Lucznikowska

The building at right is no longer there. It may have been the blacksmith shop which is shown in the 1875 atlas.

The Trusdell family ran one of the stores for many years. It was built between 1875 and 1903. Stephen Trusdell came here around 1840; his son John H. Trusdell was running the store by 1870; Lewis G. Trusdell, his brother, later ran it. Lewis was born in Amity in 1840, and died there on Oct. 30, 1909. Lewis's daughter Mabel ran the store after him.

Amity House
c. 1910
Simms Family Collection

Amity House was built between 1875 and 1903, as shown by atlas maps.

Trusdell Store Before 1903
Collection of Valerie Lucznikowska

The two buildings to the right of the Trusdell store are still standing today. The store has this configuration on the 1903 atlas map by Lathrop.

Trusdell Store Side Views After 1903
Collection of Valerie Lucznikowska

Members of the Trusdell family can be seen on the porch.

One of the topics of conversation around the checker board at the local store would have been the story of the hamlet's claim in medical history. Amity's own Dr. Henry C. Seely treated a teenage boy who had been depressed and given to erratic behavior such as swallowing household objects.

When he was unable to save the boy he did an autopsy that revealed a key, a pair of glasses, and a silver spoon in the young man's stomach. It was written up in the reports of the N.Y. Medical Society around 1853-54 and reported in the *New York Times* 5/1/1868.

The Historical Society of the Town of Warwick

The McGuffie House
c. 1900-1910
Collection of Valerie Lucznikowska

Later the property of Katie (Katherine) Clute. Mr. and Mrs. McGuffie in yard, Katie Clute seated.

The Amity Schoolhouse
c. 1905
Collection of Estella Youngman

The Amity Church School Class
c. 1900
Collection of Valerie Lucznikowska

Note how small the trees are, which today tower over the church. The bell tower was a casualty of a storm in the 1920s.

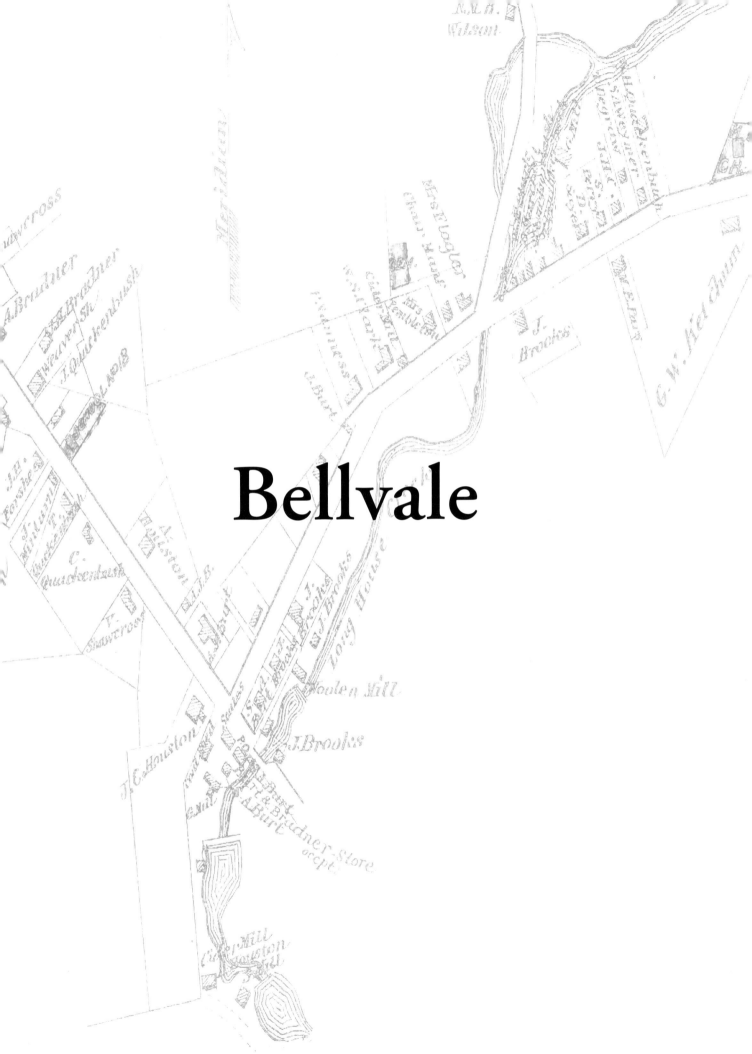

Bellvale

Bellvale

The following is adapted from Thomas Burt's history of Bellvale, *The Bellvale Rising Star*, 1907.

The hamlet of Bellvale, known in colonial times as Waywayanda, is on the lower rapids of the Longhouse Creek. The creek has its source in Upper Greenwood Lake in New Jersey. It has a large watershed at an elevation above tidewater of about eleven hundred feet, and in its descent of six or seven miles runs through several basins and down numerous rapids and falls.

Tradition accounts for the name of the stream from the longhouse that stood on its bank. The location seems to be somewhere around the intersection of State School Rd. and Lower Wisner Rd. In the fields where the land has been cultivated, plenty of flint arrowheads and large chips of flint with sharp edges have been found. In 1841, in digging a cellar for an addition to one of the houses here, the skeleton of a Native American of immense size was found, reportedly in a sitting posture.

This stream is perfect for the generation of water power for manufacturing purposes, and in colonial times was used by Lawrence Scrauley in 1745 to operate a forge or tilt-hammer plating and slitting mill. This was the only mill of its kind in the Province of New York. Once the Crown passed the Iron Act in 1750, we were not allowed to advance the manufacturing stage of iron beyond the pig and bar iron states. All usable iron had to be imported. It seems Scrauley was either prudent and shut his forge down accordingly, or else it was forcibly closed. He disappears entirely from view. In 1750 George Clinton reported that it was no longer in operation. During the war of 1812, a Mr. Peck had an establishment upon the stream, near the home of W. M. Mann, where he manufactured bridle-bits, stirrups, buckles, and saddle-trees for our cavalry, as well as agricultural implements generally.

The old forge site and the lands along the rapids up to the line of the Cheesecock Patent were bought by Daniel Burt in 1760, and soon after he built a flouring mill and a sawmill, both of which were washed away by the breaking away of the main dam during a very unusually heavy shower of rain. A flouring mill was located near the site of the earlier one. A sawmill was built in 1812 by John Bradner and Brower Robinson and rebuilt by Thomas Burt, who operated it and a wood turning shop for about twenty years. The dam was washed away and the mill was in ruins by 1907. A wool carding factory was built by Nathaniel Jones about 1810, which he sold and subsequently it was enlarged for the manufacture of broadcloths by Joseph Brooks. About 1812, James, the son of Daniel Burt, settled three of his sons in Bellvale in the milling and mercantile business. They established shops for a blacksmith, carpenter, wagon maker, and the manufacture of red earthenware pottery. Benjamin Bradner had a tannery before 1812 where the ruins of the old sawmill were. The vats were located by the old raceway and the bark was ground in a circular curb upon the flat rock back of the sawmill by rolling a heavy millstone over the bark as at one time apples were reduced to pumice by cider makers.

About 1808, the Bellvale and Monroe Turnpike was built to make a shorter route to the markets along the Ramapo River for the produce of the farmers of Warwick. It was nine miles long and shortened the distance previously traveled by about half. The road was maintained about fifty years and the charter then surrendered to the State, and the road divided into districts. A fund of about $500.00 on hand was spent in putting the road in order before the charter was surrendered to the State. The stockholders never received any money for their investment. The massive stone arch bridge that spanned the channel at Bellvale was built in 1832 to take the place of the old wooden one then unsafe for travel. The stone bridge was replaced by a modern bridge in the 1930s during the improvement of Rt. 17A.

Bellvale mountain was home to some of Warwick's earliest settlements. Joel Henry Crissey wrote of their traces in his essay *The Neighborhood That Lost:* "There were so called roads…they are dim trails now washed out and overgrown, and can only be traveled by those willing to go back to the most primitive manner of travel—one's own feet."

The Historical Society of the Town of Warwick

Main Street Bellvale
c. 1910
Historical Society of the Town of Warwick

Bellvale Store and post office on left. Looking West along 17A toward Warwick Village. This is today's Bellvale Store, the former Quackenbush store.

Bellvale Store & Post Office
c. 1905
Collection of E. Roecker

The original Bellvale Store and post office, which stood near the left side of the entrance to Mill Pond. The proprietor and postmaster for many years was Augustus J. Burt. Locals say this structure was originally the barn on the Burt homestead, and later converted. The young lady appears to be wearing a very emancipated garment — pantelletes!

Burt (Bellvale) Store
c. 1913
Collection of E. Roecker

Early stores carried many types of goods. Here we can see that they sold Jewel stoves, which advertised high fuel efficiency. Even in the old days, getting more out of home heating and cooking appliances was very important!

Bellvale Store and Post Office
c. 1915-1920
Collection of E. Roecker

By World War I the new site for the store and post office was already well established. At this time it was also a Goodyear service and gas station.

Stone Bridge at Bellvale
c. 1910
Photographed by F. J. Welles
Historical Society of the Town of Warwick

This stone bridge was constructed in 1832.

Stone Bridge at Bellvale
c. 1870s.
Collection of Florence Tate

Another view of the Bellvale single arch stone bridge that spanned the Longhouse Creek along what is now 17A. What appears to be a large old mill building is on right side. This image is taken from a stereograph by William C. Thomas.[10]

William F. Wheeler Homestead
c. 1910
Historical Society of the Town of Warwick, Joslyn Collection

Located west of Bellvale on the right side of 17A heading toward Warwick, the Wheeler homestead was purchased by Joel Wheeler before 1806. The barn was raised by a community barn raising on July 4, 1776, by Samuel Ketchum, a Revolutionary War soldier. Samuel also kept a toll gate here, for those who traveled to and from the Sterling Mines. The house was probably built by Samuel or Philip Ketchum. It burned down Feb. 2, 1909.[11]

Mt. Peter House
c. 1910
Collection of Batz Family Courtesy of E. Roecker

Opened about 1890 by Michael Batz and family, the Mt. Peter House was on the right side of the road going from Bellvale to Greenwood Lake. Mt. Peter was named for Peter Conklin, who owned the mountain land.[12]

Mt. Peter House
c. 1910
Collection of E. Roecker

"Making Hay While the Sun Shines" at the Mt. Peter House. It looks like one of the attractions that the Mt. Peter House offered its guests was hayrides!

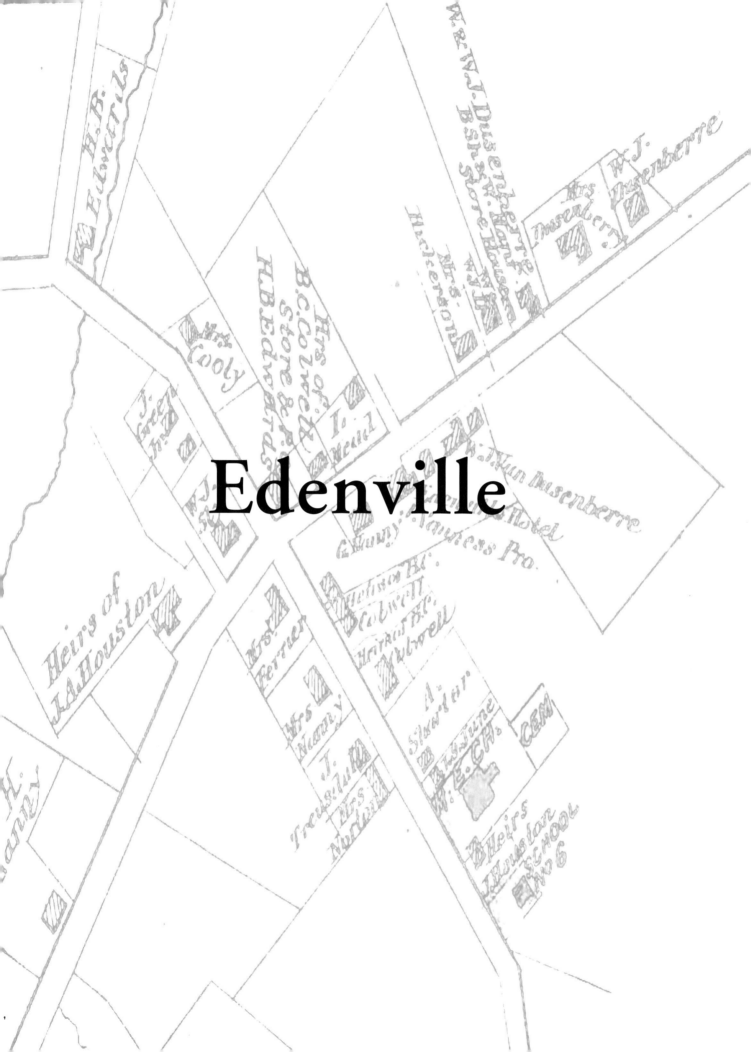

Edenville

Edenville

The hamlet of Edenville was settled first by Jacobus Post, Sr. in 1734. The next known settler was Heman Rowlee, who came from Cape Cod in 1769. They were of Dutch ancestry. The name of the community changed several times over the years; it was first known as Purling Brook, and deeds giving this name go back at least to 1765. A story is told that early Edenville landowners, Dr. Joseph Houston and Jacobus Post, Jr., once tossed a coin to determine a new name. Post won and it became Postville for a time. Then in the early 1800s Dr. James Young persuaded the residents to change the name again and it became Eden from its proximity to Mounts Adam and Eve. In 1826 it was found that an Eden already existed in New York. The Postmaster General gave them some alternate names that were not already taken, and Edenville was chosen; there were variations even after this time, however—an 1829 map by David Burr gives it the name of "Edenton."

The road through Edenville is an old route, and was used by colonial travelers. Local lore tells us that even George Washington traveled this way through town on occasions, and after he established the headquarters at Newburgh, his papers include several references to using this more western route in order to ensure safe delivery of his mail and dispatches. The Jacobus Post "Shingle House" served as an inn, and was known as the "Halfway House" between Morristown and Newburgh. The stone Heman Rowlee house, built by a Revolutionary War veteran, still stands at 4 Waterbury Rd., but at this time due to an oil spill, its fate is uncertain.

In the 1870s the Mt. Adam Granite Company contributed to the hamlet's growth, once employing over two hundred men and even supplying Brooklyn with one million paving stones, for a single contract.

On July 27, 1910, some reminiscences of Edenville appeared in an article in the *Warwick Dispatch*, excerpted here:

Before the Civil War the village held many more people than to be found here today. Then, as now, there was one church and one school house. Women wore calico dresses, sunbonnets, and cowhide shoes to church. Children came to school in droves. There were no fancy studies, the boys got whipped as regularly as they stood up to spell. There were two hotels, kept by Sam Gobel and Bill Coleman. Henry Green ran a blacksmith shop. At one time there were seven shoemakers all doing a good business. Leather was obtained at the tannery operated by the Clasons at Jockey Hollow. The shoemakers would walk over there and carry home a whole hide. Mountaineers made baskets in those days, brought them down to Edenville, and exchanged them for groceries. All freight had to be brought from Chester or Goshen. Wagons were loaded both ways. One could get a ride either way any day at almost any hour. There were several good cooper shops where churns, barrels, tubs and firkins were turned out. Wagon making was a great business. John Dusinberre and Benjamin S. Colwell were rival manufacturers. They made wagons all winter and sleighs all summer. Boys were bound out to learn a trade, serving three years. The first year they got $25.00 with board and clothes. Everybody worked from sunrise to sunset. Men who worked at a trade and lived in the village each kept a cow and pastured her on the highway. These cows kept the grass and weeds down along the roads. Farmers made butter and shipped it to New York. No grain was bought. The farms produced all that was required. Every farmer kept oxen for farm work and drove horses on the road. There was no scarcity of farm help and wages were low. Neighbors got along well together and often exchanged work. Edenville had no water power and no mill, so grain was carried to Sanfordville or Jockey Hollow to be ground into flour. There was more travel through Edenville fifty years ago than through Warwick. The railroad and other changes have turned the tide of travel and industry from the little hamlet over the hills. The quiet of a New England Sabbath hovers over it while its people dream of its past glories and rest content with present things.

Mounts Adam & Eve
1907
Historical Society of the Town of Warwick

Edenville derives its name from proximity to Mounts Adam and Eve. In earlier times it was named "Postville," but by 1829 had became "Edenton." This pastoral view is in many locations now obscured as fields return to woods or become suburban lawns. Corn stalks were stacked into shocks (right middle) to help them dry before being gathered for winter livestock fodder.

"Original" Shingle House
Before 1907
Historical Society of the Town of Warwick

Standing on Pine Island Turnpike near Union Corners Road, this was built by Jacobus Post, Sr. in 1734. This home was also run as an inn for colonial travelers. Jacobus was a prominent member of the community, serving as Town Supervisor to Orange County's first Board of Supervisors when it first met in 1798. According to a memoir of Paul D. Case published in 1898,

there were two separate rooms in the cellar, with separate fireplaces sharing a common flue that was about 6 feet square. A story is told that on the old planks of the floor was a hoofprint of George Washington's horse, which had been newly shod in Edenville that day. Jacobus had a son, Col. Jacobus Post, who died in January of 1812. The home burned on Jan. 18, 1907, and its destruction was so significant it was noted in the *New York Times*.[13]

Edenville
Before 1915
Historical Society of the Town of Warwick

Days Gone By   A History in Pictures Town of Warwick, New York 1827-1945

Bird's Eye View of Edenville
This view showing horizontal, present-day Pine Island Turnpike crossed by vertical present-day Edenville Rd.

c. 1945
Collection of John and Virginia Clancey

Edenville Panorama
Panorama of Edenville looking west toward Mt. Eve.

c. 1905
Collection of John and Virginia Clancey

Main Street Edenville
1906
Historical Society of the Town of Warwick

Main St. Edenville (Pine Island Turnpike) shows store that is now Country Dream restaurant at left. This store was founded around 1850 by Wheeler Roe. Local lore tells us that this spot was also a very early trading post in colonial days. The store passed through several owners, and is now owned by the Kenneth Henderson family.[14]

Pine Island Turnpike
1903
Historical Society of the Town of Warwick

Pine Island Turnpike, looking toward Rt. 1 from direction of Union Corners Rd. Edenville Hotel on the left.

Main Street Edenville
1906
Historical Society of the Town of Warwick

Here you can see the Methodist Episcopal Church and the school on Main Street (present-day Edenville Road). The church was organized in 1822. The school had 110 students between the ages of 10 and 16 by 1840; it was a large number,

and shows how large and busy the hamlet was at that time. The students studied astronomy, the New Testament, and mythology, in addition to the basics, according to a list of textbooks compiled in 1843.

Seely S. Everett's General Store
c. 1940
Collection of John and Virginia Clancey

The Seely S. Everett General Store in Edenville was on the corner of present day Pine Island Turnpike and present-day Edenville Road. Notice the "dead man" on the left. This block of concrete reads, "Slow, Keep Right" in order to direct traffic safely. At one time the store was owned by Rev. H. R. Edwards, called by his clerical title "Dominy," who toiled at the store six days a week and wore a tall white silk hat. From 1878-1883 the store belonged to James W. Houston. George S. Everett, father of Seely Everett, took over the store in 1883. He did a thriving business due to the Mt. Adam Granite Company, which he supplied with a two-horse-wagon load of merchandise twice a week. It passed through other hands before Seely S. Everett acquired the store in 1912 and ran it until 1949. Mr. Everett remembered when carloads of flour and freight were carted from Florida or Pine Island, taking several days to haul. The advent of electricity, refrigeration, and furnaces made life much easier. Men gathered for a game of cards or dominoes and exchanged home-spun yarns and chatter of the day.

Seely S. Everett's General Store
c. 1930s
Collection of Warwick Methodist Church Gift of Hazel Miller

The Seely S. Everett General Store is now home to the Country Dream restaurant. Seely Everett bought it in 1912 and operated it until 1968, when the Henderson Brothers purchased it.

Houston Farm
c. 1930s
Collection of John and Virginia Clancey

Snowstorm on the Houston Farm, 262 Pine Island Turnpike. Prior to 1793 the center section of this house was a tavern providing a rest for busy travelers in and through Edenville. It was later converted to a home and remained in the Houston family from their purchase in 1793 until sold in 1978. The center section, the earliest part of the house, retains its wide board beaded edge paneling.

Nanny Homestead
c. 1900
Collection of Don and Kathryn Lomax

Family members at the Nanny homestead, 4 Blooms Corners Road. The home later became the Edenville Inn restaurant and then a private residence again.

Waterbury House
c. 1940
Historical Society of the Town of Warwick

The Heman Rowlee "Waterbury House" sits at 4 Waterbury Rd. The stone portion of the home was built by Rowlee, a Revolutionary War veteran and mason by trade, in the 1790s. Heman (not Herman) is a biblical name. Many years later it became the home of James Waterbury, and he added the frame part of the home. A story is told that Almeda Waterbury and Charles Williams were married here around 1890 in the maple grove at midnight amid festive lanterns and elaborate floral decorations. The garlands from their wedding hung for thirty years after in the attic. About three years ago an oil spill in the basement made the house unlivable, but it is hoped that further cleanup operations will save this historic home.

An Edenville Snowstorm
c. 1930s
Collection of John and Virginia Clancey

Edenville blizzard's depth on Pine Island Turnpike is shown by the snowdrift relationship to the height of the horses.

Date uknown
Collection of John and Virginia Clancey

John Wright Stevens House
c. 1910
Collection of John Wright Stevens

Located at 254 Pine Island Turnpike, this early farmhouse was owned by J. Tompkins in 1859, by heirs of B. C. Colwell in 1875, and by G. S. Everett in 1903. The original house, c. 1825, had one room on each side of a central staircase. This section has sash-sawn chestnut beams and wide board floors. Additions were put behind the house in two stages and the front was updated in the style of the 1860s. This photo was taken after renovations were complete.

Inside Everett's Store
c. 1940
Collection of John and Virginia Clancey

The interior of Everett's Store displays a Thanksgiving Special: Daisee Fancy Pumpkin and Flako Pie Crust for 25 cents.

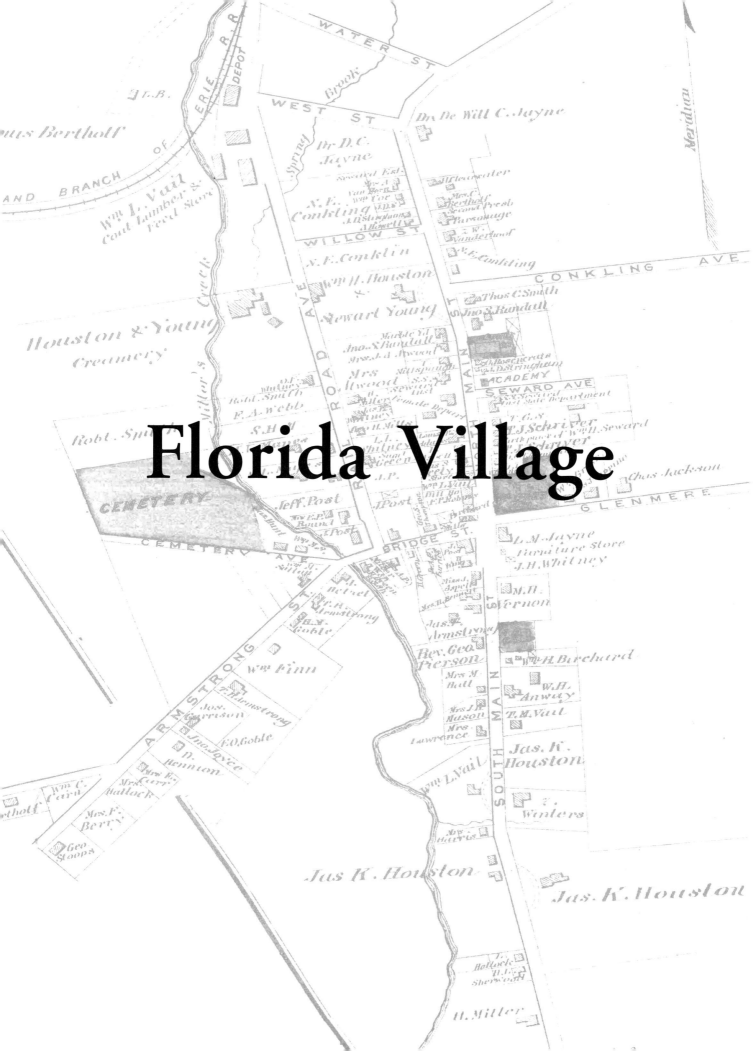

Village of Florida

The following is adapted from the Florida Historical book, *Florida, New York, Orange County : An Early Look at its Faces, Places and Winding Staircases* published by The Florida Historical Society © 2002.

Florida was originally named Brookland because the village was situated at the intersection of two streams. Although it might have been called Florida as early as 1738, it wasn't until the 1760s that a meeting was held for the express purpose of changing the name to Florida. The name comes from the Latin *floridius aetas*, which means covered with flowers. According to the then young William Thompson II, provisions for a dinner to follow the meeting were brought from Newburgh and the young village was duly christened. As quoted in *History of Orange County* (by Samuel W. Eager, Esquire c. 1846), "In the hilarity of the festival, they christened the place 'Florida' and drank down the pretty maiden name in flowing bumpers."

Three Florida mills have been researched and documented. As early as 1740, the two Randallville Mills on the northern edge of the Village of Florida formed the industrial site known as Silva Glen and the Mill in the Glen. The third prominent mill with a rich history was the Zebulon Wheeler Gristmill and Sawmill, situated near the intersection of Spanktown and Big Island Roads.

During the Revolution, Florida was an important corridor for the movement of troops, supplies and prisoners from southerly positions such as Philadelphia to northern strategic positions such as Albany and parts of New England. Florida was an important stopover as there were taverns, including the Kennedy Tavern, blacksmiths for wagon repair and horseshoeing, wheelwrights, fresh water, food, and other supplies.

In 1742 the people of Florida built a meeting house, later called the First Presbyterian Church. Methodism began to interest Florida residents in 1831; while the church initially grew, it declined later in the century. Not long after the Civil War, many Polish people immigrated from Europe and settled in this area of New York. These deeply religious people needed a priest who spoke their language, and they organized the building of the parish of St. Joseph Roman Catholic Church in 1895. In 1887 St. Edward Roman Catholic Church was established as a mission church of St. Stephen's Roman Catholic Church, Warwick.

The two most prominent Florida citizens were Samuel Sweezy Seward and his son William Henry Seward. Locally, it was the father Samuel who was the most influential. Dr. Seward was a medical doctor, postmaster, New York State Legislator, county judge, and judge of the Court of Common Pleas. He established a mercantile business, became a shrewd financier, kept a farm and owned a fleet of schooners. In 1812 Florida was divided into school districts. Five one-room schoolhouses and the larger Washington Academy served the community for many years; however, Seward was never completely satisfied with them. In 1845 he decided to establish his own "Institute" of higher learning that still exists today.

Nationally and internationally the most influential citizen was S. S. Seward's son, William H., who progressed through various elected governmental posts and achieved lasting fame as Secretary of State in the cabinets of presidents Abraham Lincoln and Andrew Johnson.

The volunteer fire department was founded in 1885. The Florida Water Works came into being in 1892, the Florida Telephone Company was formed in 1901, and electricity came to Florida in 1910. The Village of Florida was incorporated on August 5, 1946. However, that incorporation came very close to reality about 50 years prior to that 1946 date.

The Historical Society of the Town of Warwick

Main Street, Florida
1939
Collection of John and Dorothy Kimiecik

This view of the Florida Village begins, on the left, with a Gulf gas pump outside the Dill House, 8 North Main Street. It is followed by the Vail Hotel and Wm. L. Vail's country store. At the end, on the right, is W. Muetschele's (Piekarnia) Bakery, 21 North Main Street. Displayed across the road is a banner announcing the first Onion Harvest Festival.

South Main Street
1930
The Florida Historical Society

South Main Street, Florida, is pictured beginning on the left with just the edge of the two-story covered porch of the M. B. Tallman Millinery Shop. Several stores follow, including Vernon's Apothecary before South Main is crossed by Bridge Street on the left and Glenmere Avenue on the right.

Post Office & Confectionery Store
1900
Reprinted from Florida Historical book [2]

The lower left portion of this building, built prior to 1875, was used as the Florida Post Office for the late 19th century and the first half of the 20th century. The lower right portion was a confectionery store. Standing in front of the Post Office are Mr. and Mrs. Vandenburg and Daisy; in front of the Confectionery is Susie Matthews. On the balcony are Mattie Woodruff and Lucy Murray.

Florida's General Store
1920-1930
Reprinted from Florida Historical book [2]

Florida's General Store, at 2 North Main Street, had many owners except during World War II. William Rosenberg altered the exterior appearance and introduced a modern supermarket to the area. He named it the Victory Supermarket and later renamed it the Big V.

Florida Street Scene
c. 1905
The Florida Historical Society

An old Florida street scene begins with the Aspell House on the left.

The Dill House
c. 1915
Reprinted from Florida Historical book [2]

The Dill House, built in 1838 by Justus Dill and his brother William at 8 North Main Street, Florida, housed a restaurant, hotel rooms, meeting rooms and a ballroom. Designed to meet the various needs of the many travelers on the busy road through the village, the front porch, balcony, and windows were perfect for watching Fourth of July celebrations, which were traditionally held in front of the Presbyterian Church. Balls, sociables, and country auctions were held regularly at the Dill House.

Dill House Garage
c. 1930
Reprinted from Florida Historical book [2]

Farries "Dutch" Gorish, an excellent mechanic, operated the garage at the Dill House. Herb Crookston is pictured with Gorish in this photo.

Florida Street Scene
c. 1905
The Florida Historical Society

Another Florida street scene looks south and features the Aspell House with cupola in the center.

Days Gone By   A History in Pictures Town of Warwick, New York 1827-1945

Seward Homestead
c. 1886
Reprinted from Florida Historical book [2]

This 1886 drawing represents the 1797 Seward family home, formerly at 35 North Main Street, Florida. Dr. Samuel S. Seward came to Florida in the late 1700s, shortly after his marriage to Mary Jennings of Goshen. Their son, William H. Seward, was born in this house in 1801. The birthplace was dismantled and the timbers and lumber were used to rebuild it at right angles, behind its former location.

Professional Building
c. 1860
Courtesy of the Seward House, Auburn, NY

S. S. Seward built his second home at 62 North Main Street, today the Professional Building, in 1812, primarily in the Federal Style. It is marked by an oval gable window with decorative tracery. Originally the two-story frame building had yellow painted clapboard with green shutters. The front door was centered with a three-pane transom and sidelights. In later years it was the female department of Seward's Institute.

Updated Seward Homestead
c. 1900
Reprinted from Florida Historical book [2]

This 1887 Victorian Gothic Mortimer Mapes house replaced the old birthplace. It has patterned shingles, a snub roof turret, barge boards, and fine detailing.

Nanny Homestead
c. 1915
Collection of Suzanne Straton

Harrison W. Nanny's house, c. 1890 right, was remodeled in the early 1900s by Dr. Felix Villamil to house his family and his office at 37 North Main Street, Florida. He rebuilt it in the Spanish style, reflecting the doctor's birthplace in Navia, Asturias, Spain.

Hardware Store & Tin Shop
c. 1880
Collection of William and Audrey Howell

This 1880 photo of 42 and 46 North Main Street, shows Louis D. Adams standing on the front porch of his Hardware Store and Tin Shop.

Florida National Bank
c. 1915
Collection of John and Dorothy Kimiecik

The Florida National Bank at 59 North Main Street was built on the site of the Washington Academy in 1911. The idea for organizing a bank was first brought up by Samuel Green, who died before the plan was carried out. The bank was reorganized and the name changed to The National Bank of Florida in 1933. Notice the World War I "V for Victory" sign in the window.

Conklin(g) Homestead
c. 1930
Collection of Bob and Nancy Scott

The Nathaniel E. Conklin(g) house, located at 107 North Main Street, was built before 1859. Twin bay windows are incorporated into a wrap-around porch supported by framed columns. A bay window looks out from a second floor bedroom. The interior has one of two original mantel pieces, slate with faux marble grain paint, fitted for parlor stoves.

George Washington Seward House
1875
Historical Society of the Town of Warwick

This home was built in 1847 on the west side of Main Street by G. W. Seward (1808-1889), who was the brother of William H. Seward, Secretary of State under Abraham Lincoln. It was later owned by Stewart Young. This engraving appeared in *Atlas of Orange County* by F. W. Beers.

Dr. Jayne's Office & Homestead
c. 1911
Collection of John and Mary Fish

Built by Dr. DeWitt Clinton Jayne in 1842, this picturesque-style house was constructed at 121 North Main Street using timber from a local swamp, bricks made at Vernon's Brickyard and granite from Mt. Eve. The doctor's office was located in the basement. This photograph was taken on September 25, 1911, at the birthday party of Elizabeth Roe.

Vernon Homestead
c. 1897
Reprinted from Florida Historical book [2]

The Montgomery H. Vernon house, c. 1890, is located at 33 South Main Street. It is a classic Queen Anne/Victorian style house with much detail still intact. Montgomery H. Vernon was a manufacturer of brick in Florida and also operated an onion shipping concern and a meat business. Note the Methodist Church building on the right side of this photograph and the windmill behind the house.

DeKay (Vernon) Homestead
c. 1926
Reprinted from Florida Historical book [2]

This photograph of the Vernon Homestead, was taken during the ownership of Clarence and Elizabeth DeKay. George S. Vail, Jr., brother of Elizabeth Vail DeKay, is on the roof.

Dr. Mars' Office
c. 1925
Reprinted from Florida Historical book [2]

This c. 1859 house with mansard roof became the second home and office of Dr. Jesse D. Mars. Located at 36 South Main Street, the front door has glass panels and the interior retains many fine features including marble mantels. Don DeKay is riding a pedal car in front of this home.

Dr. Mars' Home and Office
c. 1940
Reprinted from Florida Historical book [2]

This c. 1830 house, formerly located on the corner facing South Main Street was moved to 6 Glenmere Avenue facing the Presbyterian Church. In 1903 it was owned by Dr. J. D. Mars and used for many years as both his home and medical office. This picture was taken in 1939 or 1940, shortly before the barn on right was taken down.

Sears Roebuck House
c. 1925
The Florida Historical Society

This house at the right, on South Main Street, is said to be one of the Sears Roebuck houses that were ordered from the Sears Catalog.

Houston Estate House
c. 1900
Reprinted from Florida Historical book [2]

This homestead, 72 South Main Street, was part of a large estate. It was built by S. Houston approximately 1830, and was enlarged in 1871. At one time during the Vail ownership, two unmarried sisters lived here. One supposedly had a seafaring suitor whose visits are recorded by date, under the marble mantel.

Schultz Farm
c. 1915
Reprinted from Florida Historical book [2]

This 149 acre farm, 156 South Main Street, was purchased in 1853 by Joachim Ontario Schultz, who had been a manager of the Lorillard estate in Tuxedo Park, New York. Joachim's son, Charles E. Schultz, was born on the farm in 1856, and he continued to farm after his father died in 1898. He was educated at S. S. Seward Institute and later served as its president.

Mabee Homestead
c. 1923
Collection of Robert and Robyn Schloicka

Built approximately 1890 by the Mabee family, this clapboard house, 49 Highland Avenue, has a fieldstone foundation and has been in the Sloat family since 1900. This photo shows three Sloat children: John, Dorothy, and Harold. Local residents remember when the Sloats had a slaughter house set up in the barn. The small smokehouse is still standing on the back edge of the property.

Goble Farm
c. 1890
Collection of Jan and Elizabeth Jansen

Located at 161 Glenmere Avenue, the Goble Farm (c. 1800) originally consisted of 120 acres of land with a large dairy barn, three-story carriage house, several maintenance barns, and a corn crib. The foundation of this salt box house is of cut limestone and the four fireplaces still have exposed original brickwork. On the ground level, a large fireplace faces a c. 1800 cooking fireplace with a side-wall bake oven.

Meadow View Farm
c. 1900
Reprinted from Florida Historical book [2]

Howell's Meadow View Farm is located at 449 Route 17A. The Howell family has resided in Florida since the early 18th century, and this homestead, c. 1733, is owned today by the tenth generation.

During the years 1733-1970, as families grew and finances allowed, the house that started out as a kitchen with two bedrooms over top expanded to the thirteen-room Colonial home shown at right.

Vandervort Farm
c. 1910
Reprinted from Florida Historical book [2]

The C. Vandervort Farm, c. 1850, was formerly on the corner of Route 17A and Edward J. Lempka Drive. During the ownership of Wm. J. Roe, the outlet from Glenmere Lake was dammed to create a large swimming "pool" and beach.

Bridge Street Bridge
c. 1905
Reprinted from Florida Historical book [2]

The Bridge Street Bridge in Florida spans Miller's Creek, later called Quaker Creek. The house in the center is located at 4 Highland Avenue.

Boyd Homestead
c. 1905
Reprinted from Florida Historical book [2]

This c. 1859 home is located at 11 Bridge Street. As the photograph shows, this house once had a side-wrap porch like 7 Bridge Street. Seated on the porch are Mary Edith Green Boyd and her daughter, Mabel Boyd (Embler).

Green Blacksmith & Carriage Shop
c. 1940
The Florida Historical Society

The Green Blacksmith and Carriage Shop, located at 15 Bridge Street, was erected in 1848 by Henry Green on the bank of Miller's (Quaker) Creek. The shop extended for a distance of about seventy feet. Only a small portion of this original building still exists.

Greenwood Lake

Greenwood Lake

Extracted from the research of Wilbur Christman and Steven Gross

The first people to call Greenwood Lake their home were the Minsi or Munsee, the northern band of the Lenape tribe. They established a village called "Quampium" at the northern end of the lake. At that time the lake was much shorter, so that location is now under water. The earliest documentation of them we have is old deeds, which were surveyed by William Roome around 1874. Their habitation here was for many years, as shown by the quantity of broken pottery found by F. J. Welles and others along the lake shore. One account we have of contact is that of George Ryerson, whose grandson related in 1881 that George as a child would go with his father to the rock shelter at Awosting to barter and trade with remaining tribe members, around 1800.

After the Cheesecock Patent was signed in 1702, Dutch settlers found their way into the valley and established a community in the area north of the lake that we call "Dutch Hollow" today. Another early account that we have of this hamlet is in the mid 1800s, in Henry William Herbert's *Warwick Woodlands*. He mentions visiting the Teachman family, who resided in the Dutch Hollow area.

During colonial times the lake was smaller than today and was known as "Long Pond." It continues under this name on maps up until the early decades of the 1800s. The first dam erected that increased its size was around 1766 by Peter Hasenclever, a German entrepreneur who established the Long Pond Iron Works along the river to the south of the lake. He erected a dam across the outlet of the lake so that he could better control water flow to the works. Another dam was constructed in 1837 by the Morris Canal and Banking Company, enlarging the lake to its present size. The valley was still sparsely settled; residents included the Cooley family, whose daughter Maria married the Hudson River School artist Jasper F. Cropsey. He painted many beautiful scenes of Greenwood Lake during his time here.

Around 1856 Solomon Caldwell purchased property, speculating that this now very large lake could become a tourist destination and resort. It had been the haunt of sportsmen for several decades, but accommodations were somewhat "rough and ready." He planned to increase the lake's visitors through commercial development. The population gradually grew, and a great boom in tourism occurred when the Montclair and Greenwood Lake Railway was built in 1875. The railroad brought visitors by the carload to the eastern shore, where they were ferried to their destinations. The golden age of wonderful hotels and steamships had arrived!

Up until now, the community was a hamlet of the Town of Warwick. But as it grew, so did demand for services and amenities. With a mountain making access to Town services difficult at times, the villagers decided to create their own incorporated Village, which voters approved on March 20, 1924. Since that time the New York end of the lake has had its own governing body, providing many needed services.

The lake has attracted numerous famous visitors and residents over time, and still does today. Baseball great Babe Ruth came often, and boxers such as Joe Louis and "Sugar" Ray Robinson trained here in the 1940s and 1950s. Vaudeville legend Joe Jackson lived here and operated a restaurant. The mountainside community of Greenwood Forest Farms was founded in 1919, the first resort community of African Americans in our region, and the black intelligentsia of the New York metro relaxed here in summer. The colony hosted such luminaries as Langston Hughes.

The Great Depression had a profound impact on the lake, as people had less money for resort going; the train stopped running in 1935, and there was a quieter time for the village to adjust and grow. Over time many of the summer residences were converted to year-round homes. Gradually the community became a mix of permanent and summer residents. In warmer months it is still a mecca for water sports enthusiasts. Proximity to Sterling Forest State Park and the Appalachian Trail makes Greenwood Lake popular with nature lovers as well, yet the Village still retains its small town appeal and charm.

Hanging Rock
c. 1910-1919
Collection of E. Roecker

Hanging Rock at Bellvale Mountain, Route 17A, was a local landmark that moved from view when the road bed changed (now can be seen in the woods on the uphill side of the road). The house at center right still stands, but the roadway is on the opposite side of the house now. The rock was also known as "Drunkard's Rock" after a local legend in which a man returning home inebriated is caught by his wife and is "petrified" at the spot.[15]

Greenwood Road (17A)
1919
Historical Society of the Town of Warwick

Photo shows car on Greenwood Road (now 17A), with Greenwood Lake in the background, Bellvale Mountain on the right. As early as 1906 Warwick was looking to the state to help with improving this important connection. In typical bureaucratic fashion, the first improvements were approved by 1906, but we were still waiting for the project to be

funded, "number ten on the waiting list," in 1907. This scene was probably how the road looked after that project, until more improvements came down the pike in 1932.

Road Work on Route 17A
Early 1930s
Historical Society of the Town of Warwick

Photo shows road work on the Greenwood Lake side of Bellvale Mountain, Route 17A. A Model A Ford is parked to the side. The improvement of this precarious passage was undertaken several times. This scene looks like part of the Works Progress Administration (WPA) project. Hills, turns, and various trouble spots in the road were removed, making the road much safer, if a bit less picturesque.

Native American Pottery
c. 1933
Photo by Frank J. Welles
Reprinted from Warwick Historical Papers No. 2, Part 2

Historical Society of the Town of Warwick

We cannot tell the story of Greenwood Lake without mentioning the first residents, the Native Americans who made the lake and its valley their home. A tribe of Minsi Lenape had their village, named "Quampium," at the north end of the lake, about where the present village is. An early collector of artifacts, photographer Frank J. Welles, over many decades, assembled a large collection of pottery shards, all gathered near the lake. These are some of his collection.

Iroquois Pot
c. 1932
Photo by Frank J. Welles
Reprinted from Warwick Historical Papers No. 2, Part 2

Historical Society of the Town of Warwick

A spectacular find was made by Maude Storms on a ledge of rock west of the north end of the lake—a huge intact pot. It was identified as Iroquois in manufacture, perhaps obtained in a trade with the local tribe. The Minsi or Wolf Clan were the northernmost branch of the Lenape, with Iroquois settled fairly close by. We are told that the pot was in the collection of the Museum of the American Indian in New York City at the time this article appeared. A well known rock shelter is also along the lake, near the southeastern end of the lake, in New Jersey.

Greenwood Lake Main Street
c. 1910
Collection of Nina Steen

Main Street as it was many years ago.

On September 25, 1959, the Village Historian, Doris Ragone, wrote an article in the *Greenwood Lake Buzzer* about life in the Village in the old days:

> *Our sleepy picturesque village looked very different in 1924 than it does now. Shady trees lined the dirt roads and only a few automobiles were seen…on the corner across from the Parish House was Minturn's General Store, and this was the hub of activity. It was more than a country store. It was the "club house," a meeting place for friends and neighbors, a bank, where checks could be cashed, and a place where Pa could leave the kids when he had a job to do. On the side of the store hung a bulletin board. On it were notices about socials, elections, etc. Out front there were some benches where older men could "set" and visit by the hour…but come winter, they would move inside and gather around the iron pot pellied stove, glowing cherry red from the fire.*

Windermere Avenue
c. 1915-1920
Historical Society of the Town of Warwick

Windermere Avenue at the corner of Waterstone Road, facing south.

South Windermere Avenue
c. 1915
Collection of Nina Steen

Windermere Avenue facing south, Greenwood Lake Department Store on left.

Winter in the Village
c. 1903
Collection of Barbara Morgiewicz

For the cold months of the year, the Village was a quieter community; winter sports included a toboggan run, a ski area, and ice boat sailing and racing. The hotels still provided employment, as most had their own ice houses and needed them stocked well for the comfort of their guests in the heat of summer. This shows the East arm area.

We have ample stories of earlier times at the lake, including those told to a *New York Times* reporter by Joe Woodruff and printed on 1/7/1877:

> *The first white settler was one Belcher, who had land at what is now Brown's Hotel. His sons migrated to the northern end, which land his descendants hold by livery of seizin'.*

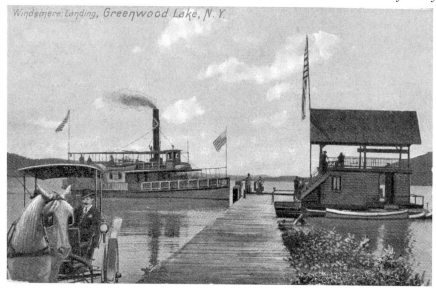

Windermere Landing, North end of Lake
c. 1915
Collection of Nina Steen

Waterstone Landing, East Shore
C. 1915
Collection of Nina Steen

Edward Waterstone and family arrived at the lake in the 1860s. His wife, Martha Sharps, was the daughter of Edward Sharps, for whom the "sharpshooter" was named. They and their family ran Waterstone Cottage for many years, located at the east shore.[16]

The Steamer Montclair
c. 1880-1910
Collection of Richard Hull

The Steamer Montclair was the largest of the steamers and apparently the only side-wheeler. The three steamboats on this page were run by the Greenwood Lake Transportation Co. Often packed with visitors as it churned up and down the lake, it was retired to DeGraw's landing and quietly decayed.

The Steamer Arlington
c. 1915
Collection of Nina Steen

Steamer Arlington ferried rail passengers from the Sterling Forest Station to their hotels. After many years of neglect, the Arlington sank at dock near the Waterstone bridge.[17]

The Steamer Milford
c. 1915
Collection of Nina Steen

After carrying many vacationers to their destinations and back to the station again, the Milford was eventually dry docked at Sterling Forest, then removed in the 1970s.

Family Fun
c. 1914
Historical Society of the Town of Warwick

Photo of unknown landing at Greenwood Lake shows families enjoying the lake. Family outings have been a popular pasttime for over a hundred years.

Houseboat on Greenwood Lake
c. 1915
Collection of Nina Steen

Windermere Recreation Park
c. 1915
Collection of Nina Steen

Windermere Recreation Park was at the head of the lake, in the general area where the Village of Greenwood Lake Public Beach is now.

Greenwood Lake Park
c. 1915
Collection of Nina Steen

The Boulders
c. 1915
Collection of Nina Steen

Located at 99 Shore Avenue, The Boulders is listed on the National Register of Historic Places. J. Pierpoint Morgan built the house in 1912 for his organist, who he thought would be inspired by the beauty of the lake. Unfortunately, the poor man was terrified of snakes, making it necessary to suspend his bed from the ceiling by chains!

Dr. Gudewill's Castle
c. 1915
Collection of Nina Steen

Rudoph H. E. Gudewill, a NYC physician, built the castle for his wife in 1903, reportedly fashioned after his father's castle in Germany. The next owners were the John Tiedemann family, whose adopted son "Sonny Connors" was the grandfather of the current owner— Yankees' great Derek Jeter.[18]

Lake (Lawton)

Main Street Lake, New York
c. 1910
Collection of Marty Feldner

In earlier days, the hamlet of Lake, New York, was known as "Lawton." The name was changed to Lake in 1900 to avoid confusion with Lawton, Pennsylvania. Situated between Sugar Loaf and Wisner, it was the community center for the Warwick farms on the lake and near the Chester border. This photo shows Main Street (Lake Station Road) looking toward Kings Highway.[19]

Simms General Store & Post Office
c. 1910
Collection of the Simms Family

The general store of John A. Simms also served as the post office from 1864 to 1934, when the post office was closed. It stood on Lake Station Road near the crossing (see above).

Ostrom Homestead (Brookside Farm)
c. 1915
Collection of the Simms Family

The Ostrom Residence on Bellvale Lakes Road (Brookside Farm) shows a typical country lane scene at Lake. You can almost hear the crickets droning in the summer afternoon as you walk barefoot down the dusty dirt road. The quiet agricultural community became livelier after the arrival of the railroad.

Webb Farmstead
c. 1910
Collection of the Simms Family

Mr. Webb's residence was a well kept farmstead. Even patriotic holidays did not interrupt essential chores such as doing the wash.

Lake Station Depot
c. 1910-1915
Collection of the Simms Family

The Lake Station depot served as a pickup point for dairy and farm products that were being shipped to market, as well as a convenient place to board the train into town.

Railroad Workers
c. 1915
Collection of the Simms Family

Railroad workers at the Lake Station depot get ready to move to the next work location on the handcar.

Little York

The Legend of Little York

By Susan M. Yungman, adapted from *Usu Leut* newsletter, Winter 1981

Little York was settled in the late nineteenth century by a group of Volga Germans. These Germans had left their homeland to settle in the Russian Volga Valley. They did so at the invitation of the Russian Empress, Catherine II, in 1763. They left Germany to avoid religious persecution, high taxes, and the devastation of their farmland following the Seven Years War, which thrust them into extreme poverty. Once in Russia, their settlement was restricted to the Volga Region, and they were expected to become farmers. Closed German villages were established. The Empress authorized building a church in each colony, paid for by the government and repaid by the colonists. Four years later the Empress issued a set of instructions regulating every detail of their lives.

Conrad Luft was one of the Volga Germans who decided to leave Russia and venture to a new land. He had served in the Czar's army, and it was a time of great upheaval and change in that country. It was in 1888 that Mr. Luft, his wife, and a baby daughter left the village of Jagodnaja Poljana, Russia, and made the long difficult journey which brought them to the port of New York.

While they were detained at Castle Garden, (the arrival point for immigrants prior to Ellis Island), Mr. Luft was offered a job on a farm in Orange County, New York. This brought him to the area now known as Little York, which was mostly forest at that time, with only one other house in the immediate area. About a year after Conrad settled here, another daughter was born and named Katherine, the first baby born in Little York of Volga German immigrants. The Lufts managed to make a living and eventually wrote their friends and relatives in Russia telling them of this fine country and pleasant prospects. Soon family and friends followed Conrad's suggestion and they too made the long trek to America. With the help of Conrad and early clergymen, more immigrants found their way to the Little York area, including his good friend August Youngman, who had also served in the Czar's army.

They cleared the timber from the swampland and found the soil around Little York to be rich, black (somewhat like the "chernosem" in Russia), fertile, and most suitable for growing onions and other vegetables. They had no money with which to purchase land, so they went to work wherever they could find employment. Many worked for the railroad company, some for established farmers and land owners, and others were carpenters. After they saved enough money to make a down payment on some land, they bought virgin land, cleared the forests, made improvements, and after much struggle and hardship, it did become a "land of milk and honey" for them.

During those early years, many families who came to the Little York area from Russia later moved on to various Western States. Conrad Luft himself later went to Oshkosh, Wisconsin, a pioneer there as well, but his daughter returned to Little York after she married John Scheuermann, and raised a large family here. Some of the families who remained in this area were: Schmick, Leinweber, Schadt, Scheuermann, Luft, Lust, Daubert, Pfaffenroth, Gerlitz, Ruhl, Rudy, Weitz, Langlitz, Mohr, Schlagel, Eurich, Wagner, Ochs, Ott, Miller, Wilhelm, Sircable (Zurgiebel), Kleveno, Kiel and others. Some of them were from the villages of Pobotschnaja and New Straub, but most of them came from Jagodnaja Poljana.

Die Kirche (The Church) was always the focal point of the social and family life of "Our People" (Usu Leut). By 1898 land was purchased and a German Lutheran Church was started. In 1901 the congregation was incorporated, a pastor was called, and eventually the church was completed. This building was destroyed by fire on Christmas Eve, 1918, but a beautiful new edifice was erected in 1918, and to this date many descendants of the Volga Germans still worship here. Probably the biggest social event in Little York is the annual "Sauerkraut Supper" which is held at the Church hall every October and features fresh ham and "prie," German rye bread, and other traditional delicacies. Little York has always been a friendly place—like one big family—where people share each other's joys and sorrows.

Scheuermann & Ruhl Funeral
October 20, 1917
Collection of St. Peter's Church

Photo taken at funeral of Philip Ruhl and Harry Scheuermann. The tradition of photographing the dead was common at this time. For those of lesser means, often this would be the only photograph taken of the deceased, and family members wished to have a remembrance. The original church building is shown; it burned down a short time later.

Daubert Funeral
c. 1918
Collection of Emilie Scheuermann

John Daubert's funeral was held on the farm at Little York Road. The photo was given by the wife of the deceased's grandson. The family is of German and Russian descent.

Little York Lutheran Parochial School
c. 1926
Collection of Emilie Scheuermann

The Lutheran Parochial School in Little York was located on Little York Road. Pictured above in front row, second from right is Louise Daubert. In the second row, third from the left is Herman Scheuermann.

St. Peter's Lutheran Church Confirmation Class
c. 1917
Collection of St. Peter's Church

A confirmation class at St. Peter's Lutheran Church. The church played a great role in the little community, and confirmation was a passage to young adulthood. These farm families pulled out all the stops to provide proper dress for this important day. Shown are (left to right, standing): Elizabeth Gerlitz, John Schmick, Henry Pfaffenroth, unknown. Seated: Anna Sayer, Marie Langlitz.

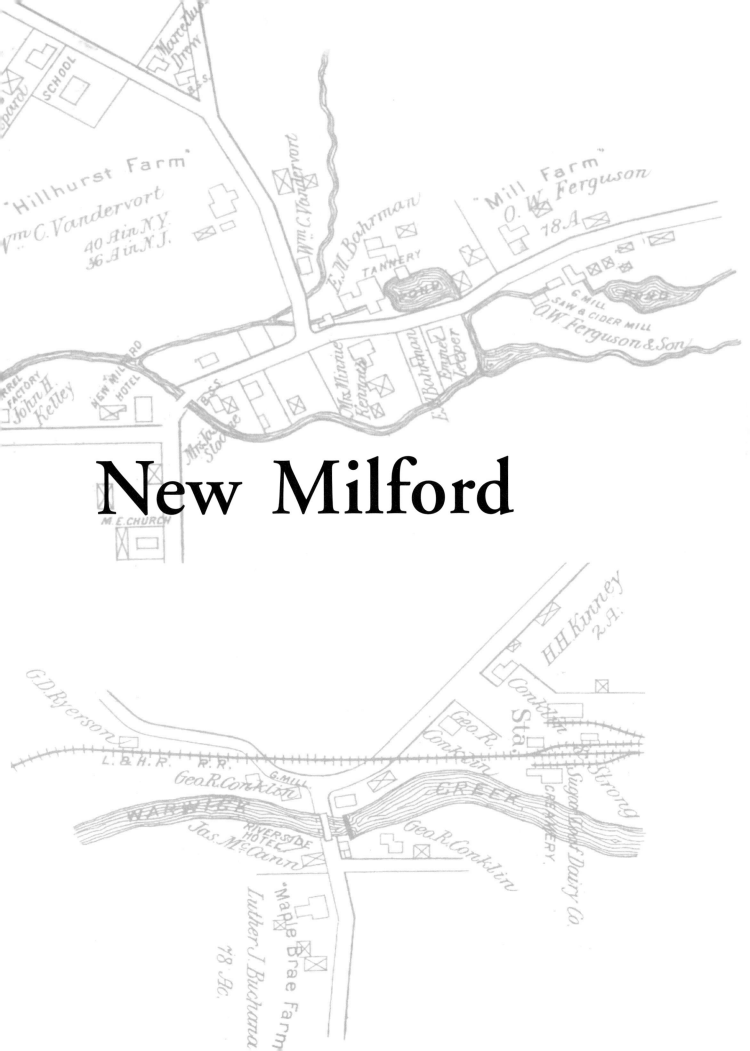

New Milford

New Milford

Compiled from historic accounts and the work of Terry Hann

The land containing the hamlet of New Milford was deeded to Cornelius Christansie as part of the Wawayanda Patent in 1702. It changed hands several times, then was purchased by Thomas DeKay and Benjamin Aske in 1724. In the earliest days there were only two or three dwellings here. These early homes included that of Cornelius Lazear, Sr. on Iron Forge Road, which was also run as a tavern.

The Wawayanda Creek and the Doublekill provided ample power for early mills and factories beginning around 1770. These included an iron forge owned by Col. John Hathorn. In 1802 John Lazear built a grist mill and a factory for making axe and shovel handles. New Milford was a very busy place in the first quarter of the 1800s, with six mills on the Doublekill, four on the brook nearby, and two mills and a distillery on the Wawayanda. A post office was begun in 1815, with the first postmaster being Merritt Coleman. A boarding school for young ladies was opened in 1835. The Minisink and Warwick Turnpike was part of the main route from New York to Port Jervis and it ran just north of the hamlet's center, contributing to the growth and prosperity of the little community.

The early name for New Milford was Jockey Hollow, and various tales about the name have been told. According to Mary Bahrman McPherson in 1946: "It seems that in the old days a favorite pastime of the neighborhood farmers was to race their steeds between the old Inn…past the church on the quarter of a mile level stretch of road which afforded a fine race track. Some of these farmers owned very fine horses. They would return to the Inn to talk things over, sometimes swap horses and probably do a little betting." It may be that some of the residents objected to being identified in this manner; we can see from studying old maps that at some point before 1829 the name "New Milford" had been adopted.

In 1859 the following businesses paid to be listed in the *New York State Business Directory* by Adams, Sampson & Co.: James Sloan, blacksmith; Thomas Harrison, carriage and coach maker; Demarest & Lazear, grist mill; Clark & Thompson, grist mill; Robert DeKay, hotel; John Keiran, hotel; Lewis Wood, house and sign painter; Charles Wilson, physician; Samuel Clawson, tannery; John Reiran, Jr., woolen goods manufacturer. On the map by French and Beers of the same year there are also two saw mills and a distillery.

When the call went out for volunteers to fight in the Civil War in 1861, even though New Milford had only 150 citizens, they sent 28 men; one in five of the residents marched off to the battles in the South.

A great fire swept through the business section of the hamlet in 1898, destroying many of the stores. According to Mary McPherson, "The life of our community proceeded in these peaceful channels until March, 1898, when a fire destroyed the center of Jockey Hollow including the village store and post office, hotel, five dwellings and a store house. The place has never recovered from the shock of that terrible fire. That was forty-eight years ago and only the store has been rebuilt by J. B. Stanaback, the present owner." Another huge fire swept through in March of 1900. Nearly fifty years later, the business center was still struggling.

Businesses that hadn't been burned continued to thrive, however; Borden's had established a creamery here in 1905, and by 1908, it processed and shipped 4,500 gallons of milk daily.

In 1929 state funds were appropriated to complete a new road through New Milford, straightening some of the old twists and turns, and this more direct approach is today's Rt. 94. Recent construction has established a wider area for the hamlet's business center.

Despite challenges and changes, New Milford residents have a keen sense of their identity as a community, and there is a history of meeting and discussing current topics at the store, which has stood in the same spot in the center of the hamlet since the 1800s. In the 1940s the group was known as the "Cracker Barrel Committee," and they published reports in the local paper.

New Milford Covered Bridge
c. 1870
Historical Society of the Town of Warwick

The mill that is the foundation for *Pacem in Terris* is at left. The building at right is identified as a store on the 1875 Beers' Atlas map. The bridge was not covered after 1898.

Below is the same location. A succession of bridges crossed the Wawayanda at this site.

c. 1870-1898
Historical Society of the Town of Warwick

New Milford Bridge
c. 1915
*Collection of
Casper and Terry Hann*

A later version of the bridge at New Milford.

Twin Bridges, New Milford
c. 1915
*Collection of
Casper and Terry Hann*

This quaint scene of the Twin Bridges in New Milford was frequently photographed. From looking at maps, it appears it was along Route 94, between the intersections of Covered Bridge and Iron Mountain roads.

Twin Bridges at Night
c. 1905-1910
*Collection of
Casper and Terry Hann*

Twin Bridges by moonlight.

The Historical Society of the Town of Warwick

The Glen at New Milford
c. 1915
Collection of Casper and Terry Hann

The Glen at New Milford, looking upstream from below the mill pond at Covered Bridge Rd.

The Kill at New Milford
c. 1915
Collection of the Simms Family

The Kill at New Milford. This is probably the Doublekill.

New Milford Station Complex
c. 1915
Historical Society of the Town of Warwick, The Joslyn Collection

The complex at New Milford Station. Conklin and Strong's store is at left, Borden's Condensery at center rear, the station house just below Borden's, and the freight depot is at the right.

79

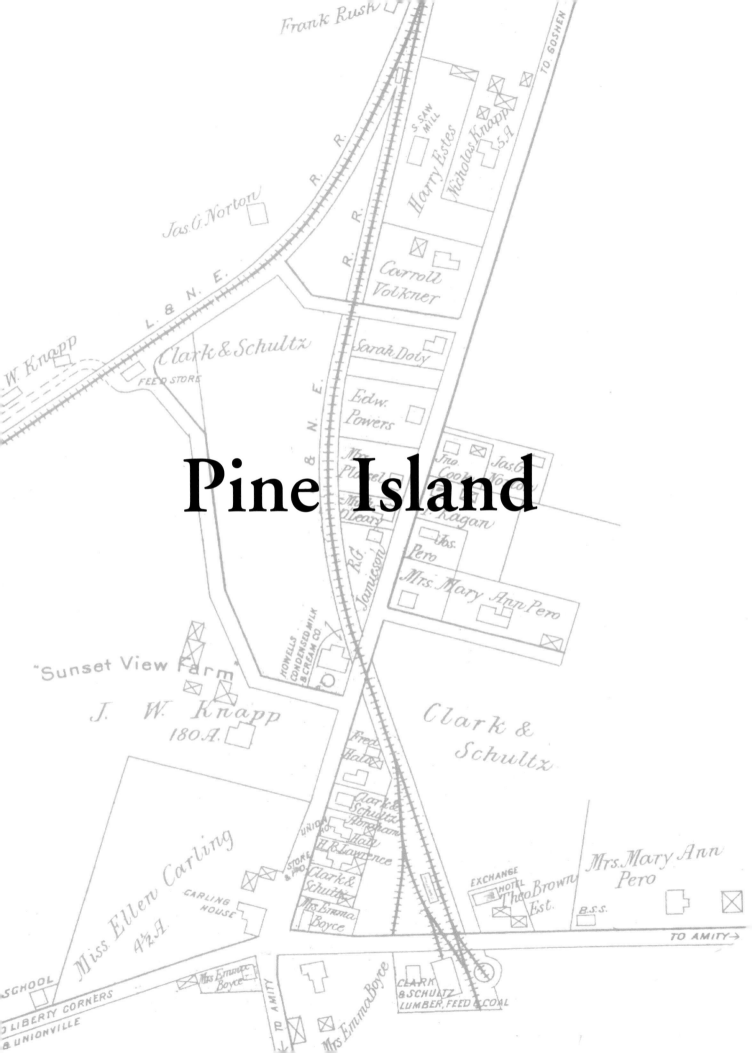

Pine Island

Adapted from the work and archives of Frances Sodrick and *Drowned Lands of the Wallkill* by James Snell

Pine Island is so named because until the mid 1800s this knoll and the others around it were often completely surrounded by water. The Black Dirt region was a vast marshland that stretched for over 40,000 acres. The region was a habitat for many species of animals and migrating waterfowl, and had been a hunting ground for eons, as shown by the abundant Native American artifacts found here. Remains of prehistoric animals such as mastodons have also been discovered. The higher ground was forested with trees such as Pine and swamp loving species such as the now rare Atlantic White Cedar. The country surrounding this great swamp was settled at a very early date. The settlers called the flood prone tract "The Drowned Lands of the Wallkill." Author Henry William Herbert ("Frank Forester") wrote many hunting tales in the mid 1800s about the abundant wildlife that inhabited the area.

During the dry season the islands were reached without great difficulty, and the wild grass that grew on the marshy meadows afforded excellent food for cattle. Owners of drowned land derived considerable revenue from renting out pastures to the cows of neighboring farmers. Through the summer season thousands of cows were turned upon the grassy meadows. Sudden floods frequently came, however, and the water rose so rapidly that many cattle were lost annually before the herdsmen, in boats, could drive them to the uplands. The cows that reached the island were kept there until the water had subsided. The main duty of the farmers' boys in the early days was to watch the cattle feeding among the treacherous Meadows of the Drowned Lands. Diseases from the mosquitoes inhabiting the swamp were a continual threat.

As early as 1797, the *American Gazetteer* notes that "the channel might easily be deepened, as to prevent the land from being drowned, and the people from sickness." By 1804 the drowned lands owners, believing that by altering the course of the Wallkill River, and removing certain of the obstructions in its bed, the lands would be drained and large portions of them made tillable. The project proved harder than expected and attempts continued for many years, finally with some success in the late 1820s. As a result of changing the channel, however, the mills of the New Hampton area had their water cut off, and a long struggle over water flow became known as the "Beaver-Muskrat War." During the time of drainage, sickness from malaria type diseases carried by mosquitoes increased dramatically.

A settlement was made at Pine Island very early, and the little community grew. The first store was run by Judge Bradner and Sandy Baron, about 1820. S. E. Gale had established his business here in 1838, with partners George McDaniels and W. Cuddeback. William Wilcox was running a hotel in 1859. In November of 1869 a station of the Erie Railway connected to the main line at Goshen was opened, and farmers could ship their dairy products more easily. The post office was established in April of 1870 with S. E. Gale as postmaster. Businesses that were operating by 1880 included Gabriel Carlin's hotel, S. E. Gale's lumber and coal yard, and Charles H. Woolsey's general store.

According to Wilmot Vail, writing in 1909, Pine Island was a route on the Underground Railroad: "Sometimes fugitives arrived on foot and sometimes a friendly conductor of a railroad would help them on their way. There was a man named Wood, the owner of a brickyard at Pine Island, who helped those who were closely pressed by their pursuers to hide or forward them on their journey" (a clipping of this account is in a scrapbook donated to the Society by Henry L. Nielsen, Jr.). Mr. Vail was one of the "conductors."

In the late 1800s, Polish immigrants who were brought to work on area farms recognized the value of the rich, black soil, and began renewed efforts to successfully drain it for year-round usefulness. In 1878 a 600 acre piece of the swamp was given to the Mission of the Immaculate Virgin for the Protection of the Homeless and Destitute, in New York City. The "Mission Land" as it became known was not cultivated, however, until 1905, when a Polish priest from Florida convinced the Sisters to sell it for $11.00 an acre. This newly available and inexpensive land increased settlement by Polish immigrants, and their generations of toil and perseverance have made Pine Island what it is today, a major agricultural resource.

The Historical Society of the Town of Warwick

Pulasky Highway & Route 1
c. 1922
Collection of Barbara Morgiewicz

Pulaski Highway corner at Pine Island looking West. Location is just north of the corner of Route 1. Shows the creamery, which burned down in recent years, and the access road down to the Clark & Schultz feed store.

Weeding Onion Fields
c. 1930
Collection of Barbara Morgiewicz

Weeding in an onion field.

Big Island Road
c. 1915
Collection of Gary and Kathy Randall

83

Days Gone By   A History in Pictures Town of Warwick, New York 1827-1945

Harvesting Onions
c. 1930
Photo by Msgr. John Felczak
Collection of Barbara Morgiewicz

Pine Island Creamery The Pine Island Creamery, which stood on
1922 Pulaski Highway just a short distance from
Collection of Frances and Bob Sodrick Route 1, burned down in 2001.

J. W. Knapp Homestead
c. 1915
Collection of Barbara Morgiewicz

The J. W. Knapp house stood on a knoll off Pulaski Highway, which has since been removed.

General Store
c. 1915
Collection of Barbara Morgiewicz

Broadway (Pulaski Highway) in Pine Island. The store at left is the general store that stood near where the present gas station stands.

Seely General Store
1945
Collection of Barbara Morgiewicz

The general store at Pine Island, run by W. S. Seely.

Photo by Msgr. John Felczak

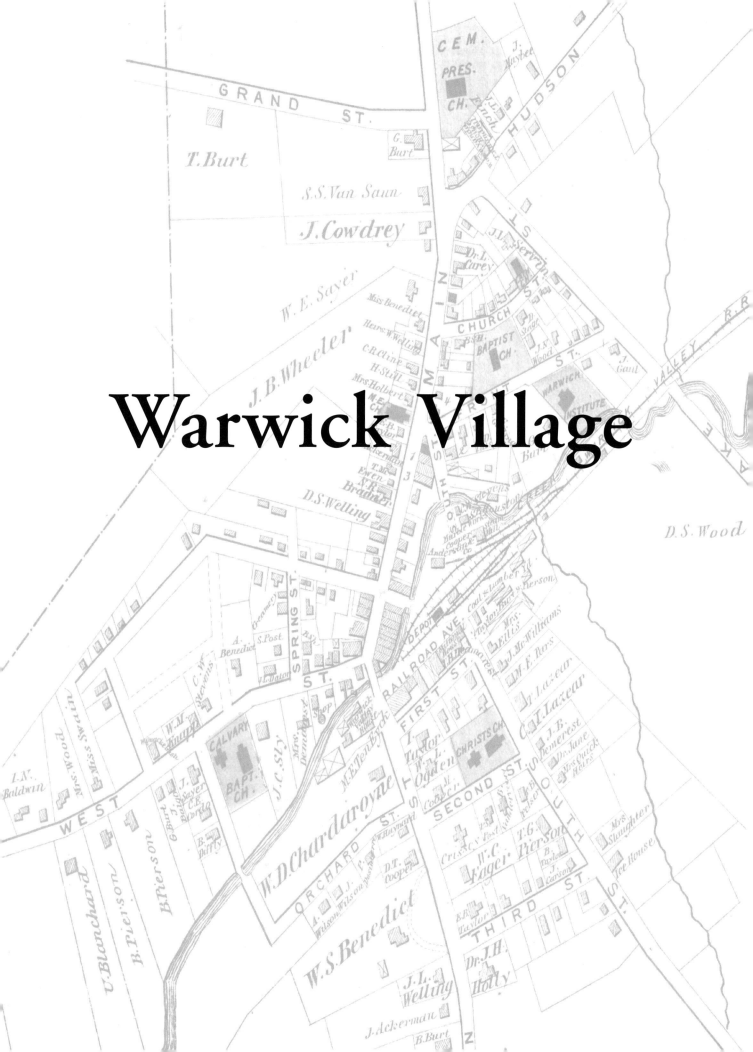
Warwick Village

History of the Village of Warwick
Adapted from the work of Dr. Richard Hull

Europeans began to settle permanently in the Warwick Valley area after 1703 when the Wawayanda patent was signed with the local Minsi Indians. In 1719, Benjamin Aske purchased a small portion of the patent and established a farm, called Warwick, from which the present village took its name. In 1735, the ancient Wawayanda Path was transformed into a colonial King's Highway and the area was more opened up to white settlement. In 1749, Colonel Charles Beardsley bought land along the Wawayanda Creek from Aske and built his home at the corner of West and Main St. In 1764, James Burt built his home, the Shingle House. And in 1766, Francis Baird erected Baird's Tavern. By this time most of the Indians had left or had become assimilated into colonial culture.

The village was emerging as a provisioning, social, and religious center for surrounding farming families, one of many hamlets in town. It was smaller than Bellvale, Florida, New Milford, and Sugar Loaf. This changed dramatically with the construction of the Warwick Valley Railroad in 1860. Within a few years Warwick was transformed into a prosperous and bustling center of commerce, banking, and retailing. In 1867 it was large enough to be incorporated as a village and to be endowed with its own government.

Amenities like a private subscription library, fire companies, waterworks, and tree-lined streets were soon established. Churches multiplied and a private school, the Warwick Institute, drew students from all over town. In 1864 the First National Bank of Warwick opened, followed eleven years later by the Warwick Savings Bank. These became powerful financial institutions that lent capital to the expanding local dairy and orchard industries. Both town and village developed a strong identity through the establishment of two vibrant weekly newspapers, the *Advertiser* in 1866 and the *Dispatch* in 1885.

By 1902, the village had its own telephone and power companies and it had taken on characteristics of a prosperous suburban community replete with many hotels, lecture halls, and ballrooms in the elegant Red Swan Inn and in the venerable Demerest House, all a stone's throw from the Lehigh and Hudson River Railway station. The village became the region's premier shopping center and a mecca for summer vacationers. In 1916 a hospital was opened, followed a year later by the Village Board of Trade. In 1927 the Albert Wisner Library was dedicated.

The emergence of the automobile age and the demise of the railroad took its toll on the village. A further blow came with the steady decline of our town's agricultural mainstay, dairy farming. In the 1950s and early 1960s business declined on Main Street, the Red Swan Inn was demolished, and many buildings fell into disrepair. The Chamber of Commerce, founded in 1939, struggled valiantly to keep businesses on Main Street from going under altogether.

A dramatic revival began in the mid-1960s, sparked by the village's spectacular centennial celebration in 1967. A new civic spirit emerged. Public parking lots were built, shade trees were planted, businesses were modernized, and historic buildings and homes were restored to their former grandeur thanks to leadership from the Historical Society, which helped place the village on the New York State and National Registers of Historic Places. Today, Warwick Village is one of the few in the state that can boast of surviving the mall-mania of the 1980s and 1990s and maintaining the integrity and commercial vitality of its central business district.

The Historical Society of the Town of Warwick

**Warwick Panorama
c. 1907**
Collection of Femi Roecker

Warwick Village panorama, 1907. Enlarged section below shows more village details.

This photo is labeled "Warwick as Seen from Near Dublin," in *The Warwick Advertiser* supplement of December 1907. It appears to be taken from the northwest, in the vicinity of the ridge around Demerest Hill (Pine Island Turnpike).

The Village was incorporated in 1867. The upper portion of the village had been settled by 1766, and its shops and businesses supported the agricultural community during colonial and Revolutionary times.

Lower Main Street was sparsely settled until the middle of the 1800s, in part because wetlands along the Wawayanda Creek bred disease-carrying mosquitos.

In the enlargement below, we can see that the Village still retains its small town charm. The spires of the Old School Baptist Church (middle left) and the Methodist Episcopal Church (now the Clocktower, right) are evident, along with some magnificent homes.

Clinton & Galloway
c. 1915
*Historical Society of the Town of Warwick
Joslyn Collection*

Part of the Samuel Welling farm was purchased around 1850 by Elihu B. Taylor, who laid out Clinton Avenue, Galloway Road, and Linden Place. Taylor sold lots to various persons who built homes there. Clinton Wheeler Wisner designed many of the homes on Clinton Avenue and Linden Place.

The Welling homestead is still surrounded by fields, but they are rapidly disappearing. At the back of this property, nearer the hills and stream, stood Mistucky, the major Lenape village at the time the Europeans arrived to settle.

Route 94 Near Galloway
c. 1910
Collection of Gary and Kathy Randall

Colonial Avenue
c. 1919
*Historical Society of the Town of Warwick
Joslyn Collection*

At another village entrance, the homestead of W. W. Van Duzer at 71 Colonial Avenue is shown around 1915. The house still stands but the barns are now gone. The home was built by William L. Benedict in the early 1800s.

Sanford Memorial Fountain
c. 1912
Historical Society of the Town of Warwick

In 1904 the heirs of George W. Sanford dedicated a fountain in his memory at the corner of Colonial Ave. and Main St. It has two sides—one for watering horses, the other for people to drink from. The crossroads had been a traditional gathering place for the community since its beginning days, and it was here we held celebrations and bid farewell to families migrating to the West, and troops moving out. The later addition of a bandstand and the Forester monument to create "Fountain Square" added to its role as the hub of the community.

Bandstand
c. 1920
Historical Society of the Town of Warwick

A bandstand was eventually erected, and concerts were held. Maintenance of the Sanford fountain proved tricky, as it needed piping and drains. Eventually the upkeep became too much, and as horses had disappeared from the scene, it was retired as a fountain. Then the bandstand became too attractive to loiterers, and it was removed.

Fountain Square
c. 1920
Historical Society of the Town of Warwick

View north to Fountain Square. The wall to the left was for the Wheeler homestead, later the home of the White family, which was torn down and the wall and knoll removed. This property was the home of Lurana White, foundress of the religious order The Sisters of Atonement (Graymoor). Currently the location is the home of Country Chevy Olds.

Days Gone By   A History in Pictures Town of Warwick, New York 1827-1945

Main Street Looking North
After 1918
Historical Society of the Town of Warwick

From intersection of Oakland Avenue and West Street. In some ways it hasn't changed all that much, thanks to being placed on the National Register of Historic Places.

Main Street Looking North
c. 1939
Historical Society of the Town of Warwick

Photo shows the Masonic building on left which was renovated between 1918 (top photo) and this photo (1939). Notice the building to the right now has a third floor with dormers and the building design flows smoothly from one to the other.

Main Street at Night
After 1915
Collection of S. Gardner

The shops of busy Main Street even in earlier days stayed open into the evening hours. One resident remembers extended hours on Saturday especially for "the telephone girls," who were brought out of the city to Camp Sherwood for fresh air in summer, and to downtown in wagons.

The Village Lamplighter

From Collection of Simms Family

Before electricity, streetlights were gas or kerosene that had to be lit and extinguished manually. In 1885, Warwick composed the following instructions to its lamplighter. In 1888, a lamplighter was paid $25.00 a month to light and extinguish all of the lamps every day.

1. Use careful judgement as to what night lights are needed. Should it be cloudy during a moonlight period, all lights are to be lighted.

2. All lights are to be burning at dark.

3. No lights are to be extinguished before 10:00 PM, and as soon thereafter as possible.

4. All lamp-posts are numbered from No 1 up, and the lighter in his monthly report to Trustees will report all cases of broken chimneys, or damaged lamps, etc.

5. Monthly report will be made out and presented at least 24 hours previous to the regular monthly meeting.

6. All chimneys and lamps shall be kept clean.

Village Lamplighter

Mainstreet in the Future
c. 1920
Historical Society of the Town of Warwick

A clever artist overlaid other images onto Main Street to create a horrifying vision of what an overcrowded Warwick would look like. Anyone who has tried to get somewhere on a Saturday or Sunday afternoon recently will find this a familiar scene!

Days Gone By — A History in Pictures Town of Warwick, New York 1827-1945

Main Street Near South
c. 1875
From "Atlas of Orange County" by F. W. Beers, 1875

This building stood where the brick store complex that houses the Toy Chest store now stands. In 1879, it burned in a spectacular fire that took nearly half of the business district with it. *The Advertiser* was located here before moving to the lower Main Street building; G. A. Miller (store on far right) was a photographer.

Main Street Looking South
c. 1915
Historical Society of the Town of Warwick

W. T. Anderson building on right was built in 1890. The business was founded in 1891 by W. Chardevoyne, W. T. Anderson, and R. L. Edsall.

Oakland Avenue & Railroad Green
c. 1910
Historical Society of the Town of Warwick

Oakland Avenue and Railroad Green look much the same today as they did back then. The Warwick Valley House, currently the *Dispatch* building, is on the extreme left. Electricity first arrived in 1898. At the corner of West and Main stood the stone house of Colonel Beardsly, who bought most of the land that is now Warwick Village from first patentee Benjamin Aske in 1749. He also built a grist mill on the stream, parts of which were still visible in 1872.[20]

West Street & Main Street
c. 1910
Historical Society of the Town of Warwick

Built around 1875, this building was home to the *Warwick Advertiser* (left) and a photographic studio (top floor, left) from its earliest days. The lower portion of the village could only become more populated after the infamous Dolson's millpond was removed. It was the cause of many mosquito-borne deadly diseases in the early 1800s, until the dam was destroyed by floods and a group of civic minded citizens purchased the property at a price Mr. Dolson could not resist. They placed a restriction in the deed that no dam could ever be built there again.[21]

Baird's Tavern
c. 1910
Historical Society of the Town of Warwick

Francis Baird built his Tavern at the junction of the King's Highway and another major travel route (now Route 94) in 1766. George Washington visited here at least once (July 27, 1782) on his way between Philadelphia and the headquarters of the main army at Newburgh. Later, it became the home of W. B. Sayer and his family. In 1991, the Tavern was acquired by the Historical Society as a museum, a gift of Mrs. Elizabeth Sanford VanLeer.

Warwick Village Hall
c. 1901-1907
Historical Society of the Town of Warwick, Joslyn Collection

The present Village Hall, which began as the Reformed Church, was moved to this location in May 1890. It had been purchased by John Dator with others and set up as stores, but in 1907 was purchased by the Village. Starting in August 1901 Goodwill Hook and Ladder shared the building (left side).

Flatiron Building
Before 1907
Historical Society of the Town of Warwick

Located at the corner of South Street and Main Street and known in past times as the "flatiron building," it has been the home of the Sanford Insurance Agency for many decades.

The Historical Society of the Town of Warwick

Post Office Block
c. 1910
*Collection of Gary
and Kathy Randall*

Forshee's Garage
c. 1939
*Historical Society of the Town of
Warwick, Otness Collection*

In this view of Upper Main Street, we can see Forshee's garage.

Railroad Avenue
c. 1915
*Historical Society of the
Town of Warwick, Joslyn Collection*

Railroad Avenue showing the Demerest House and Conklin and Strong in the background.

South Street & Old Train Station/Depot
1893-1918
Historical Society of the Town of Warwick

This view of South Street shows the old railroad freight depot on the left and the old train station at center.

The Shingle House
c. 1925
Historical Society of the Town of Warwick

The Shingle House, located on Forester Avenue, is now owned by the Historical Society. Built in 1764 by Daniel Burt, it was later occupied by Col. Garrit Post, who died March 12, 1825.

Christie-Dubois House
c. 1900
Collection of Beattie, Jacob, and May Family

The Christie-Dubois House stood on Grand Street at what is now the front lawn of St. Anthony Hospital. The well house at right was preserved and given to the Historical Society by John J. Beattie, Jr. in 1958. A well house is a little structure with a roof built over the well to protect it from falling debris, and also to protect people from falling into the well. This well house now stands in the back yard of the 1810 House museum.

Mansions: Yesterday and Today

When the railroad came to town, Warwick became a favorite summer home community for wealthy residents of New York City, bringing fortune to some of Warwick's families. The mansions still standing on Oakland and Maple Avenues preserve that "wealthy" atmosphere for us to enjoy.

Wyndhurst on Maple Avenue
c. 1930-1940
Historical Society of the Town of Warwick

Wyndhurst on Maple Avenue was built in 1896 by James A. Chamberlain, and purchased in 1928 by Mr. & Mrs. Madison Lewis. The Lewis family contributed enormously to our community. They purchased or donated funds for several of the Historical Society's properties, as well as their upkeep. This mansion stands today, and is still in the Lewis family.

This estate of Solomon W. Johnson was named "The Knolls" and is now the property of Mt. Alverno. The Franciscan Sisters of the Poor acquired it in 1924, with the intention of having a residence and a retreat house. They soon located their novitiate there as well, and established St. Anthony Hospital. A history of the property appeared in the Aug. 8, 1967, *Dispatch*.

The Knolls on Grand Street
c. 1915
Historical Society of the Town of Warwick

Benedict Mansion/Sunset Inn
c. 1915
Historical Society of the Town of Warwick

The Benedict Mansion was built by William Smith Benedict on Oakland Avenue between Orchard Street and Oakland Court. This mansion later became home to G. F. Pitts and known as "Sunset Inn." Sadly it was a victim of fire around 1950.

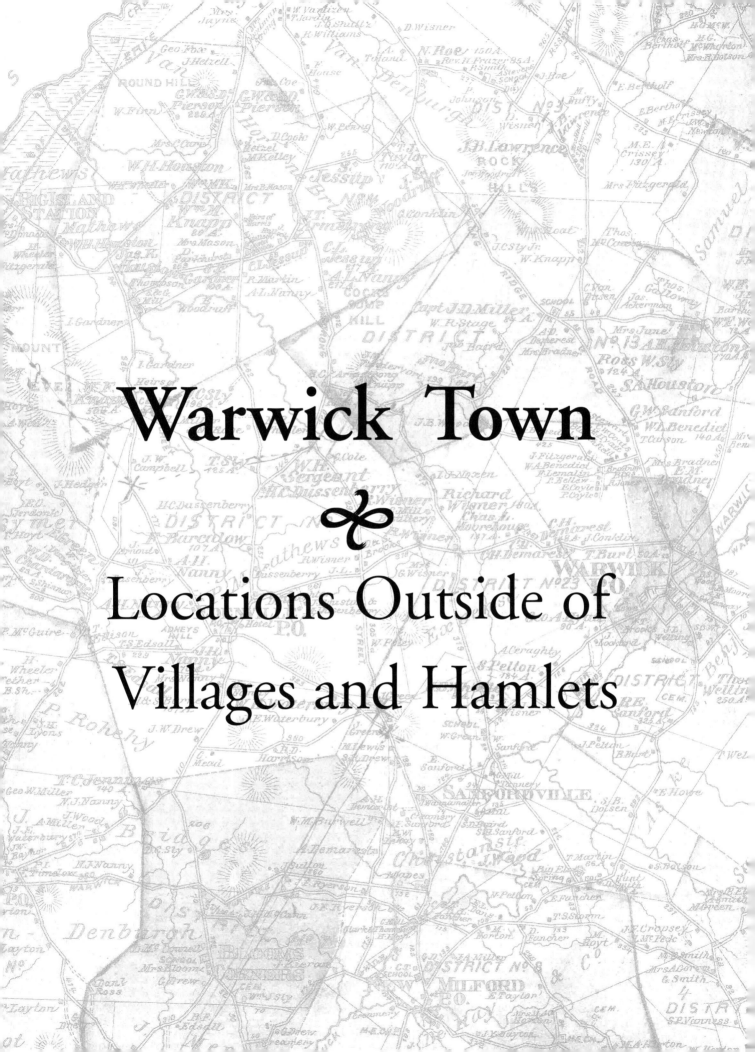

Warwick Town

Locations Outside of Villages and Hamlets

The Town of Warwick

Adapted from the work of Florence P. Tate, Town Historian

The Town of Warwick was formed by act of the State Legislature on March 7, 1788. In colonial times it had been part of the Precinct of Goshen. Its human history stretches back to the earliest documented evidence of man on this side of the Mississippi River, around 10,000 BCE. At the time of European colonization it was peopled mainly by the Minsi Tribe of the Lenape cultural group, whose ranks had already been decimated by diseases brought by the earliest explorers.

The name "Warwick" was first applied before 1719 to a farm of thousands of acres covering much of this area established by Benjamin Aske; and the designation became so well-known that it was natural to give it to the town when it was created. In colonial times, a well-traveled route passed through Warwick. The King's Highway came up the valley from Pennsylvania and New Jersey and led northeastward to the settlements along the Hudson River and thence to New England.

In its early days Warwick was settled by mainly English and some Dutch pioneers. During the Revolution John Hathorn's Warwick Militia helped guard the local area and the Ramapo Pass, and the chain that stretched across the Hudson to prevent the British from controlling the river was forged at the Sterling works.

The inhabitants of the Town met in April 1789 to elect the first Supervisor, Town Clerk, Constables, and Overseers of the Poor. From the first, for purposes of administration, the Town was divided into three districts: western, middle and eastern. For each district, an assessor, a commissioner of roads, a collector, and two fence-viewers were chosen. The Town retained its original boundaries until 1845, when the northeast corner (Sugar Loaf) was cut off to become a portion of the newly-formed Town of Chester.

A number of population centers or hamlets were in existence before the Town was formed. Early settlers made good use of the Longhouse Creek, building dams and mills and an iron forge and thus giving Bellvale its start. The Doublekill was another fine stream for water-power and mills, and there New Milford grew. The community of Florida was also established by the middle of the 1700s. During the 1800s, Amity, Edenville, and Pine Island became centers of population in the midst of the surrounding dairy, fruit, and vegetable farms. Iron mining, charcoal burning, and lumbering were occupations of settlers in the mountains from Sterling to Cascade; quarrying provided work near Mount Adam and Mount Eve. Greenwood Lake became well-known to hunters and fishermen and evolved into a popular resort and recreation area.

The town has three incorporated villages—Warwick (1867), Greenwood Lake (1924), and Florida (1946)—and many unincorporated hamlets are still called by their early names today. Some, such as "Centre," "Durlandville," "Lawton" (Lake), "Lakeville," and "Newport," have all but disappeared.

The Warwick Valley Railroad began in 1860, later becoming the Lehigh and Hudson River Railway. The railroad greatly aided the growth of local dairy farmers and other industries. It became a major travel and freight route, and brought prosperity and a "commuter" population of New York City's wealthy to Warwick. They were anxious to escape the heat and crowds of the city in summer and to raise their families in the country, a tradition which continues here to this day.

In the past several decades population surges have changed the Town dramatically, but efforts to preserve the natural resources of the Town have been ongoing, starting in the 1970s. In 1998, Sterling Forest State Park was created, containing many acres of the Town's eastern, mountainous region. Great strides have also been made to safeguard the agricultural character of the central and western portions of our community. Local, state, federal, and privately funded programs have permanently protected over 1,200 acres of Warwick farmland from development, with 800 acres more in the process of being preserved for generations to come.

The Oldest Standing House

Adapted from the work of Dr. Richard Hull

Staats Homestead
c. 1940
Photo from "Old Orange Houses, Vol. II," by Mildred Parker Seese

In 1700, Samuel G. Staats acquired about 5,000 acres of wilderness from his friend Governor Bellomont of the colonial Province of New York. The Staats family had migrated from the Netherlands to New Amsterdam in 1664. Staats himself was a prominent surgeon, fur trader, and land speculator. He had amassed a small fortune trading in beaver skins around Albany. Now his eyes turned to an area rich in game, called "Wawayanda" by the Indians, which lay closer to markets in New York City and in Europe. Dr. Staats sought the land not to farm but to exploit for fur pelts and possibly for iron ore and timber.

To strengthen his new claim, Staats built a simple but solid stone house and inscribed his initials and date "SGS 1700" on a stone just to the right of the front door. You can still see it today! The dwelling was situated over a powerful spring to ensure an internal supply of water in case of an Indian attack. The huge slabs of shale for the two-foot thick walls were dragged in from nearby outcroppings while the finely-crafted wooden beams and floor boards were probably brought by Hudson river sloops from New York.

The stone inscription was a smart move, because political upheavals in Albany in 1702 led to a change of government. Staats lost his seat on the colonial Council as well as his land title. Staats cried foul and sued. After long and bitter litigation, the court in 1713 awarded the surgeon a 13th share of the land patent, which included the stone house and much of what is today the town of Warwick. The coveted Wawayanda Patent was vaguely defined and not accurately surveyed until 1765. Later, its ownership would be argued by none other than Aaron Burr and Alexander Hamilton, who as mediators represented opposing parties.

Staats died in 1715, never having actually resided on the land. His six daughters inherited his share of the Patent and proceeded to sell it off in multiple parcels. In about 1734, some 800 acres, including the land upon which the Staats home stood, now home to Applewood Winery, was purchased by Jacobus Demarest, who trekked up from Bergen County in northern New Jersey. The land changed hands several times. Shortly after the Civil War, the farmhouse was expanded and Victorianized with a gabled wood frame second story, a rear wing, and a wraparound porch.

On June 27, 1949, the farm was purchased from Earl Predmore by Dr. and Mrs. Donald B. Hull of Ridgewood, New Jersey. The house, which had badly deteriorated, was renovated and the land was transformed from a dairy operation to an expansive commercial apple orchard under the proprietorship of Dr. Hull's son, David, who now owns and operates it and occupies the historic house.

Welling Farm
1875

Historical Society of the Town of Warwick

From "Atlas of Orange County" by F. W. Beers

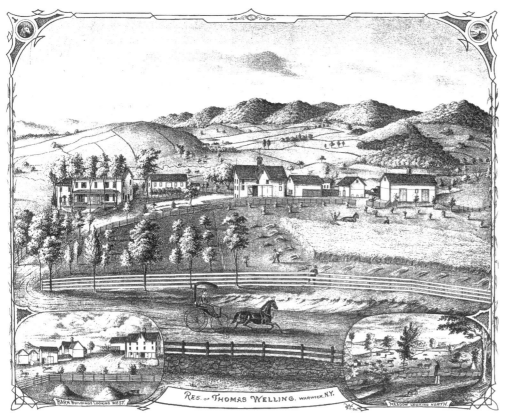

The Thomas Welling Farm is located on Route 94, just south of Warwick. Parts of the original structure were built around 1750 by Daniel Burt, then sold to Thomas Welling. The homestead is still in the family. This image is the earliest known image of the area which was known as Mistucky, the Lenape village that was present when the earliest English settlers came.

Hathorn House
1875

Historical Society of the Town of Warwick

From "Atlas of Orange County" by F. W. Beers

The Hathorn House is located on Hathorn Road near the intersection of Routes 94 and 1A. Built in 1773 by John Hathorn and his wife, Elizabeth Welling (daughter of Thomas, above). John Hathorn was a surveyor who came to help settle the New York-New Jersey border dispute of the 1700s. He taught school, was a tax collector, and became leader of the local Militia when the Revolutionary War broke out. He led local troops in protection of the Town and surrounding valleys. He was one of the commanders at the tragic Battle of Minisink and his account of that harrowing day to his superiors survives. The property is listed on the National Register of Historic Places. It was owned in 1875 by Pierson Ezra Sanford.

The Historical Society of the Town of Warwick

Hathorn House
c. 1910
Historical Society of the Town of Warwick

When John Hathorn and his wife Elizabeth built their home in 1773, they put their initials and the date into the stone gable, where it still can be see today:

H

J E

1773

Bridge at Hathorn Road
Before 1900
Collection of Bill Raynor

Photo shows the construction of the bridge at Hathorn Road by Colonel Victor Audubon Wilder, who purchased the estate that is now Chateau Hathorn before 1903. The home had been owned by Belden Burt in earlier times. Wilder made so many additions and improvements, that is became known as "Colonel Wilder's Folly." They were designed by E. G. W. Dietrich.

Sayer Homestead on Route 17A
c. 1930
From "Old Orange Houses, Vol. II," by Mildred Parker Seese

Lydia Sayer Hasbrouck
c. 1850
Collection of the Historical Society of Middletown and the Wallkill Precinct

Drawn to resemble original appearance by Townsend Sanford, this homestead was built by Daniel Sayer in 1793. The house now has a two-story wing on the right side. This homestead was the pivot of the hamlet "Sayerville," and was the home of the Sanford clan, including Benjamin Sayer.

This was the home of Lydia Sayer Hasbrouck (1827-1910). She was denied entry into Seward Institute for wearing bloomers, and took up a lifelong career of women's dress reform and suffrage.

Sanford Homestead
c. 1890s
Collection of Bill Raynor

The David Sanford homestead stood on the old Greenwoods Road. Taken in the late 1800s, this photo shows the homestead of the Sanford clan, which was built in 1765. David was born in 1711 and came to Warwick from Connecticut. They lived at this homestead for four generations before moving on to farms in the valley. Ezra, David's son, and his son, also named Ezra, lived in this house for part of their lives.[22]

Center Post Office & Store
c. 1915
Collection of E. Roecker

The post office and store at "Center" was active from Oct. 1, 1909, to Dec. 30, 1916. The first postmaster was Peter Hemmer. Center was a named hamlet very early, with School District No. 19 established there by 1813. Covering the northern edge of the Greenwood Lake valley, from Dutch Hollow up to the Monroe town line, it appears to be named for its "central" location between Greenwood Lake and Monroe.[23]

Pulpit Rock
1900
Historical Society of the Town of Warwick
Joslyn Collection

This outcrop in the field off West Street near the intersection of Route 1 has been a local landmark since time immemorial. Legends tell us that at one time, Native Americans gathered here for speechmaking—thus the name, "Pulpit Rock." The earliest image known of the rock is a stereograph that dates to around the 1870s.

Wheeler/Sandford Mill
c. 1900
Historical Society of the Town of Warwick

The mill that stood here was 102 years old in 1902. First built by a Wheeler and later owned by Ezra Sanford. Sanford operated a saw mill and tannery here as well. When it was excavated in 1929, remains of a carding machine and a fulling mill were also found. The foundation, flume, and part of the dam were washed away by a flood in 1902.

Records indicate that at least five dams were built here over the years to serve the mills. The one shown was built in 1881 by Ezra Sanford, the owner at that time. He incorporated two old millstones and had cut into the face of one millstone, "Our President died 1881. He Still Lives," shortly after the assassination of President Garfield. The sluice gates to refill the mill pond were closed on July 28, 1881, and on August 10 of that year he held a celebration for its completion.[24]

Mill Dam at Sandfordville
c. 1915
Historical Society of the Town of Warwick, Joslyn Collection

Baird Homestead
c. 1880
Collection of William Baird

The Baird Homestead has been a working farm since 1789, purchased by William Eagles Baird. Samuel Denton Baird built this stone farmhouse in 1810 on land that is bisected by Baird's Lane and Covered Bridge Road. William Baird, the current owner, is the fifth generation of Bairds to occupy the house.

In 1910 Bairds from all over the land came by train to celebrate 100 years of the Baird Homestead. They pose in the front yard.

c. 1910
Collection of William Baird

The Baird farm is probably one of the most photographed farms in America. It has appeared in dozens of national advertisements, both television and print, including McDonald's, Coca Cola, General Mills, Aramis Cologne, and NYNEX.

The mill is the only working water-powered 18th century grist mill in Orange County. A survey done in the 1990s indicates colonial building techniques, and old deeds date its existence to before 1789.

c. 1945
Collection of William Baird

Wheeler Road
c. 1899
Collection of Susan Wheeler

This old photograph shows Wheeler Road, Florida, in days gone by.

Benjamin Homestead
c. 1920
Collection of Susan Wheeler

The original c. 1779 James Benjamin homestead, 234 Wheeler Road, Florida, is a country Greek Revival structure with much interesting detail preserved including double end interior chimneys and a cut stone foundation. The house has a small hooded porch supported by four rectangular columns. This porch leads to a paneled front door with leaded glass transom and sidelights. The interior retains its wooden mantlepieces, doors, and moldings. This home was one of five nearly identical houses built c. 1779-1830 on Wheeler Road.

Gardner Farm, Spanktown Road
c. 1910
Collection of Bill Signor

This c. 1840 Greek Revival farmhouse, 34 Spanktown Road, Florida, originally served as the Samuel F. Gardner farm, along Stony Creek. It was an operating dairy farm for many years and may have been a stop for the Underground Railroad. Many original details have been carefully preserved including lights of glass above the front door, pocket doors, mahogany bannister, and two staircases.

Wisner
(Stone Bridge)

Double Arch Stone Bridge at Wisner
c. 1910-1915
Historical Society of the Town of Warwick

c. 1910-1915

Historical Society of the Town of Warwick, Joslyn Collection

The double arch stone bridge at Wisner stood for many decades at the Wawayanda Creek crossing on Wisner Road. Built in 1835 using stones from the ruins of the grist mill dam of Israel Wood (born c. 1702), it was erected in the early 1700s, and said to be the first mill in the area. Local stories tell us that he was a son of Israel Wood, Sr., Earl of Warwick (England), who had come to Long Island in the 1600s.[25]

Warwick Grange Store
c. 1870-1880
Historical Society of the Town of Warwick

The Warwick Grange Store (above) was the oldest general store in the countryside in 1957, when it was closed. Purchased by "The Warwick Grange" in 1918, and later moved across Wisner Road. The Grange was formed in January of 1913, when a Grange organizer came to speak here. The first Master of the Grange was Thomas Welling. The Grange, a rural family fraternity founded in 1867, is the nation's oldest general farm organization.

The Grange Warehouse
c. 1906
Collection of Richard Hull

Still standing today, The Grange warehouse at Wisner, which along with the other commercial buildings here, was purchased by Conklin and Strong in 1918.

Wisner Station Complex
Before 1910
Collection of Jim Murray

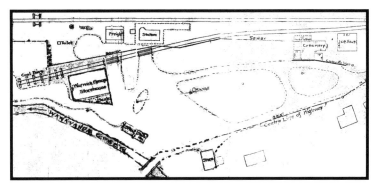

The station complex at Wisner often causes confusion; The Grange store was actually across the road from the "Stone Bridge Station" building of today. From a map of the Lehigh and Hudson River Railway property, edited for clarity.

Wisner Station
c. 1910-1930
Collection of Marty Feldner

Up the tracks from the station at Wisner, notice the old overpass bridge, which carried the road over the railroad tracks. It connected on the right side to what is now a short dead-end road, before you reach DeSanto Lane.

Wisner Family Photo
c. 1910
Historical Society of the Town of Warwick, Joslyn Collection

Wisner family members. The old stone homestead and farm is still family owned, on Lower Wisner Road. The gentleman at right with long beard is Albert Wisner, namesake of the Albert Wisner Library. He made it rich helping to rebuild Chicago after the Great Fire of 1871.

Business & Industry

The Sterling Iron Works
1736-1923

Cornelius Board secured fifty acres of land in 1736 at the southwest end of Sterling Lake from the East Jersey Proprietors, apparently acting as agent for Scottish immigrant William Alexander, Lord Stirling, so titled for his close relationship to the Earl of Stirling. This area was at that time considered part of New Jersey. During a lawsuit to settle the rival claims of the Wawayanda and Cheesecook Patents, at which Alexander Hamilton and Aaron Burr were the lawyers, James Board testified that his father Cornelius had built a bloomery and forge at Stirling Lake in 1736, which he later sold to his partner Timothy Ward. In the 1750s the Noble family also built a forge nearby. The border dispute was settled in 1769, and the Stirling area became part of New York. In 1778 Peter Townsend agreed to produce an iron chain to be placed across the Hudson River at West Point to act as a barrier for British ships. This is the second chain attempted, and was in place on April 30, 1778. The location of the successful chain was determined by a party assigned to scout out the location by George Washington, which included Warwick's own John Hathorn, a surveyor. The report was written by Hathorn. The iron works was productive for many years, under different owners, and had a surge of activity around the time of the Civil War. By 1923, the works were abandoned. The area is now part of Sterling Forest State Park.[26]

Daughters of the Revolution (D.A.R.) Marker
c. 1911
Historical Society of the Town of Warwick

Historical marker (above) erected in 1906 by the D.A.R. to commemorate the role of the Sterling Furnace in the Revolutionary War.

Lakeville at Sterling Lake
c. 1900
Collection of the Railroad and Locomotive Historical Society

A rare view of Lakeville at Sterling Lake (below), which was for many decades a thriving industrial community; little remains today.

Wawayanda Furnace
c. 1900
Historical Society of the Town of Warwick

Although the Wawayanda Furnace is in the "Moe" section of West Milford and not Warwick, its ore was carted through Warwick to New Jersey, first by oxen load (giving its name to Iron Mountain Road) and later via the L&HRR. Run by the Ames family of Massachusetts, the works contributed greatly to the local economy.[27]

Bellvale Gristmill
c. 1910
Historical Society of the Town of Warwick

The sign on the Bellvale Gristmill says "Fairbanks Scales." These platform scales were invented in 1833 and made it possible to weigh products while still on the wagon—it having been weighed empty at a previous time.[28]

Wheeler Gristmill & Sawmill
c. 1945
Collection of Elmire and Howard Conklin

The Zebulon Wheeler Gristmill and Sawmill were built shortly after 1767 on the corner of Spanktown Road and Big Island Road, Florida. The site of the mill was apparently chosen because of the confluence of two streams, which, when dammed together, produced a millpond of about ten acres to generate the power to turn the old wooden mill wheel. The Wheelers were industrious farmers and contributed to the growing community in a variety of civil offices. In 1789 Zebulon was elected Overseer of the Poor for Warwick and in 1794, a Commissioner to help with land divisions.

Bellvale Wool Mill
c. 1910
Historical Society of the Town of Warwick

The swift running Longhouse Creek provided power for the old woolen mill at Bellvale, as well as water for the mills and factories of the bustling hamlet. A fulling mill, mostly likely the same one, was founded by Nathaniel Jones about 1810, which later was owned by James Brooks. The fulling process takes the woven cloth and shrinks and binds the fibers together, making it thicker and warmer, while still very flexible and light.[29]

Bahrmann's Tannery at New Milford
c. 1910
Collection of Casper and Terry Hann

Ferguson Mill at New Milford
1907
Collection of Barbara Morgiewicz

Florida Cider Mill at Randall Street
c. 1920
Collection of Terry and Casper Hann

Notice Model T pickup truck at right.

Randalville (Randalltown), Florida

Randallville (Randalltown) was a flourishing local center of manufacturing from the mid-1700s to the early 1900s. A number of houses, stone foundations, one mill, a distillery, and a cemetery still remain from the old hamlet. Gone are the blacksmith shop, and the cider, grist, saw, and fulling mills.

The Mill in the Glen
c. 1905
Reprinted from Florida Historical book [2]

The Mill in the Glen, above at 65 Randall Street, was the eastern portion of the manufacturing center and included the millhouse that was built c. 1790 and enlarged c. 1848. The mill building (at right) was built in the 18th century and enlarged c. 1830 to house a piano forte factory. The house and mill are listed on the State and National Register of Historic Places.

Randall's Pond, Florida
c. 1870
Painted by Jasper Cropsey
(source unknown)

Jasper Cropsey painted this view of the Randall millpond, which was to the right of the mill shown above. The painting shows a mill at the far end where Great Dane Trucking is located today. The white c. 1790 house, 77 Randall Street at the right, was an 18th century inn or tavern.

Covered Bridge Road Gristmill
c. 1910
Historical Society of the Town of Warwick
Joslyn Collection

This mill's foundation is now part of *Pacem in Terris* at New Milford. The mill was built in 1863 by Squire Clark and Charles Thompson. Clues to its location include the fact that on the right side of the tracks is a hill that doesn't show in this cropped image; also, the pully support at the peak, the position of the chimney, and the shingle siding match that of the mill shown in photos of the bridge, just out of sight on the left.[30]

Enlargement of photo above at left shows more details. The mill is shown on Beers' *Atlas of Orange County, 1875,* and appears to be part of the "Clark and Thompson" complex of stores. This railroad crossing was among the most dangerous in Town, as given witness by accident reports transcribed from the newspapers by Terry Hann.

Why would a gristmill need four floors?

The diagram at right shows how a typical grist mill of this size would operate. The water moved the waterwheel or turbine at stream level, which then converted the power through a series of shafts and belts, to turn the grinding stone on the first floor. Grain was unloaded and weighed, then fed into a hopper that carried it to the top floor for feeding down into the grinding stone and then to the bagging station. The Covered Bridge Gristmill apparently loaded from the top two floors, and grain was hauled up using the block and tackle which was supported by the overhang on the roof.

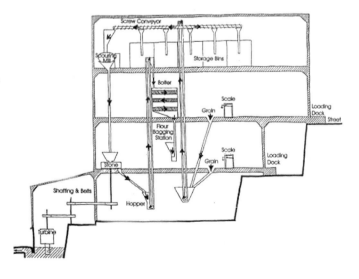

The Historical Society of the Town of Warwick

Greenwood Lake Ice House
1891
Collection of Bill Raynor

Below: Enlargement

Inset: Castle Tavern
c. 1930s
Collection of Randall Stearns

Two ice houses stood on the eastern shore, one near where the Castle Tavern is, which appears to be the one shown. The ice industry was an important one for many decades of Warwick's history, primarily for the local market until railroads made transporting to urban areas more practical. This business was established in 1864 by the Ringwood Company. Two were built, each of which could hold 45,000 tons of ice. They were about 60 feet high and covered around an acre. The business was later operated by Mountain Ice House of Hoboken. The conveyor was powered by steam, and there were five large rooms, each with a "door" that ran from floor to ceiling, which allowed the conveyor to rise to the height of the ice stacked within. When train service ended in 1935, it spelled doom for the business, which was closed in 1943 and the buildings torn down in 1945.[31]

The photo at left is not Greenwood Lake, but the method they used is shown well here—the ice would be scored by a draft horse dragging a blade, then a chunk of blocks would be split off and floated to the ramps.

At right is a portion of a 1903 atlas by J. M. Lathrop showing position of ice house, just above the state line and Sterling Forest Station.

123

Ice Pond at Meadow Road in Florida
c. 1900
Florida Historical Society

The Pine Island Creamery (Borden's) stood on Pulaski Highway a short distance from the corner of Route 1. Warwick's connection to the Borden company dates far back. John G. Borden came to Orange County in 1877 to organize a branch. The company was expanding rapidly, and bought out many of the local creameries while also building many more. Ties to Warwick were made in 1928 when they acquired the J. M. Horton Ice Cream Company. The manager of Horton's was Edward B. Lewis, who had married the daughter of Mr. Horton and settled in Warwick. A creamery was built in 1906 by Borden's. In this winter scene you can see wagons are full of ice to be unloaded into the building using the conveyor at left.[32]

Borden's Pine Island Creamery
1922
Collection of Barbara Morgiewicz

Pine Island Creamery
Before WWI
Collection of Barbara Morgiewicz

Borden's Florida Condensery
c. 1905
Reprinted from Florida Historical book [2]

Borden's Condensery, formerly on Railroad (Maple) Avenue, Florida. A condensery is where fresh whole milk is concentrated by evaporating 60% of its water.

Borden's Pine Island Creamery
1912
Photographed by James Razey
Collection of Barbara Morgiewicz

The building on the right side of the photo to the right is the condensery. The wooden ramp between the two buildings was used to transport ice from the building on the left to the condensery on the right.

Borden's New Milford Creamery
c. 1910
Collection of Casper and Terry Hann

Days Gone By   A History in Pictures Town of Warwick, New York 1827-1945

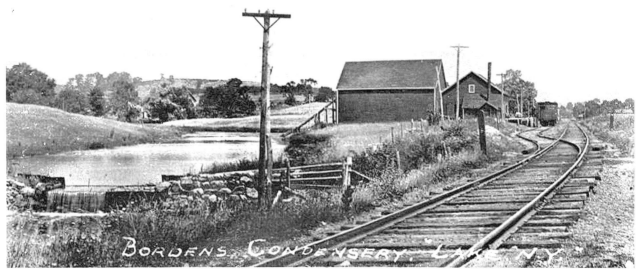

Borden's Lake Condensery
c. 1915
Collection of Marty Feldner

The Borden's Condensery at Lake was located just south of Lake Station Road, between the tracks and Kings Highway, where a patch of woods today hides all trace of its existence.

Borden's Warwick Plant
c. 1964
Possibly by Roy Elston
Courtesy of Richard Hull

The Borden's plant on Spring Street in the Warwick village. The original creamery had burned down around the 1920s, and was rebuilt.

Milk Chocolate Factory
c. 1920-1930
Courtesy of E. Roecker

The Milk Chocolate Factory located at Wisner was built by Conrad Haaren in 1916. It was originally a 30' x 60' frame building. Conrad established the Warkill Valley Milk Products Company in 1905 at Wisner. He was a native of Lubeck, Germany, born in 1866.[33]

The Historical Society of the Town of Warwick

Vernon Brickyard in Florida
c. 1898
Collection of The Florida Historical Society

Above and at right are photographs of the Montgomery Hale Vernon Brickyard at Meadow Road in Florida, which show bricks being made in large quantities. They were carted by wagon to nearby villages where brick houses were built.

Montgomery Hale Vernon
c. 1890
Reprinted from Florida Historical book [2]

Montgomery Hale Vernon was a manufacturer of bricks in Florida and also operated an onion shipping concern and a meat business.

127

Fabric Fire Hose Company
c. 1900
Collection of Raymond Hose Company

The Fabric Fire Hose Company, located at Howe & Factory streets, was one of Warwick's largest industries. It was founded by James Gillespie, one of the first inventors of seamless woven fire hose. Raymond Hose Company is named for its executive, who donated one of the buildings for their use. The company produced several inventions, including an improved tubular seamless loom which was patented by mill employee Mrs. Addie Pont in 1880. While an economic boon, this business may be the reason that during the early 1900s Warwick was known for its resistance to industrial growth; one can envision the smoke and disagreeable odor that hung in the valley from the process of lining the hoses with rubber. In 1902, the company moved to Sandy Hook, Connecticut, citing the need for more space and tax breaks as its reasons for relocation.[34]

Howe & Factory Street
c. 1915
Historical Society of the Town of Warwick, Joslyn Collection

The scene surrounding Howe and Factory streets was very different around 1915.

Warwick Knife Company
c. 1908
Historical Society of the Town of Warwick

After the hose factory moved, some of the buildings became the home of the Warwick Knife Company. Here the workers are shown in 1908.[35]

The Historical Society of the Town of Warwick

Warwick Knife Factory
c. 1910
Historical Society of the Town of Warwick

The Knife Factory was started up in the spring of 1907, and was bankrupt by January 1929. Warwick Knife Company blades are collectibles today.[36]

Machine Shop
c. 1910
Collection of the Simms Family

Around 1910, Mr. Richardson operated the machine shop on Spring Street at the corner of McEwen in Warwick. John Deming had a milk store there for years, and then Allen Ainsworth had Thunderbird Electronics Manufacturing company there.

Seely General Store
c. 1945
Collection of Frances and Bob Sodrick

The Seely General Store, which stood for many years at the intersection in Pine Island, was later purchased by the Piasecki family. Stanley Piasecki and his children operated it as a general grocery store until the late 1950s. The structure was then taken down, and rebuilt by Louis Poloniak, Sr. in the early 1960s and is better known today as Ray's Exxon Service Center. The gas station was owned and managed by Ray and Helen Shuback until their retirement in 2002.

129

Cowdrey Building
1851
Collection of Robert Eurich

In the early and mid 1800s, the center of Warwick village was at Main Street and Colonial Avenue, north of Baird Tavern. Here you see the building that stood between Baird's Tavern and the Hoyt house (now Key Bank); presently a parking lot. This building was used by a number of businesses: as a general country store by several proprietors: Edmund Reynolds in 1805, by Dr. John I. Wheeler from 1832-1836, then by John Cowdrey, and next by the partnership firm of Wm. E. Sayer and Wm. Hynard. Later John Cowdrey ran it again as a store, and in 1859 he built a house that stood here in the late 1800s; and in 1865 he tore down this old store building.[37]

New Milford Main Street
c. 1910
Collection of Richard Hull

Trusdell Store in Amity
c. 1875
Collection of Valerie Lucznikowska

Conklin & Strong Store at New Milford
c. 1918
Collection of Casper and Terry Hann

George H. Strong was born in 1867 and came to Warwick in October of 1891. He partnered with George R. Conklin and they built the New Milford plant in 1898. The business flourished and they established stores at New Milford, at Wisner, and in the Village of Warwick.[38]

Conklin & Strong Store at New Milford
c. 1920
Historical Society of the Town of Warwick

Conklin & Strong Truck
c. 1930
Photo by McKinney
Collection of Simms Family

Lazear Furniture Store & Undertakers
c. 1880
Collection of Lazear-Smith and Vander Plaat Memorial Home

The building on West Street was erected in 1876 by C. T. Lazear.[39]

Roe Brothers Inc.
c. 1940
Reprinted from Florida Historical book [2]

Roe Brothers Inc. at 65 Maple Avenue in Florida was identified on the 1875 farm map as the Wm. J. Vail Coal, Lumber, and Feed Store. Incorporated in 1886 as Roe Brothers and recorded on the 1903 farm map as Roe Brothers Inc. The photograph at right, documenting storm damage, was taken in the 1940s. Shortly thereafter, the brick and clapboard building was torn down and replaced with the present structure.

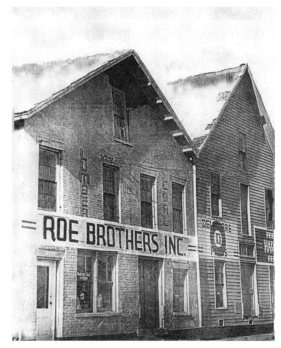

Ehler's Garage
c. 1925
The Florida Historical Society

Ehler's Garage was located on the corner of Farries Avenue and North Main Street in Florida. Farries Avenue was named after Dr. A. P. Farries, one of Florida's two physicians during the early 1900s.

At right, four gentlemen display their "catch of the day" in front of Ehler's Garage.

W. Muetschele's Bakery
c. 1905
Reprinted from Florida Historical book [2]

W. Muetschele's Bakery was located at 21 North Main Street, Florida. On the right side of the building there was a sign reading, Piekarnia Bakery (piekarnia is Polish for bakery).

Forshee's Garage
c. 1925
Reprinted from Florida Historical book [2]

Forshee's Garage was originally the home of the Florida Auto Company. The building, no longer standing, was located where the firehouse is today on Main St. Florida.

Forshee's Garage
c. 1930
Collection of John and Dorothy Kimiecik

The sales department in the interior of the garage.

Kerosene Lights on Main Street Florida
c. 1890
Collection of William and Audrey Howell

Notice the kerosene street lamp, on the left in front of L. D. Adams Hardware Store and Tin Shop. Home on the right is at 46 North Main Street, Florida. The "old lamplighter" was Garfield Vanderburgh. According to those who remembered him, Garf Vanderburgh always whistled as he swung along Main Street at dusk. Clifton Sprague had the less romantic but very important chore of putting the lights out at daybreak.

Crawford's Store
c. 1935
Florida Historical Society

In 1903, the L. D. Adams Hardware Store and Tin Shop at 42 North Main Street in Florida was expanded, remodeled, and renamed "Crawford's Store" by C. C. Crawford as is shown in this photo.

Crawford's Store Interior
c. 1935
Florida Historical Society

This interior photo of the Crawford Store provides a glimpse into the past.

The Historical Society of the Town of Warwick

Vernon's Apothecary
c. 1900
Reprinted from Florida Historical book [2]

Vernon's Apothecary was once located on the southwest corner of South Main Street and Bridge Street, Florida. Charles Vernon began his life's work here in 1883 at age 17, working for John C. Gridley. He passed his State Pharmacy Board examination in 1887 and purchased Gridley's business. At the time of his death in 1948, he was the oldest active pharmacist in New York State.

Vernon The Pharmacist
c. 1910
Reprinted from Florida Historical book [2]

Vernon is pictured at right on the porch of his Apothecary in Florida. The years of his practice saw very few changes in the corner drug store. The interior is presently displayed in Museum Village of Smith's Clove.

M. B. Tallman Millinery Shop
c. 1925
Reprinted from Florida Historical book [2]

The M. B. Tallman Millinery Shop was located on the first floor of this building, built c. 1905, at 24 and 26 South Main Street, Florida. In addition to hats, fancy dry goods and notions were sold here. The most interesting feature of this house is the second-floor covered porch.

Vail's Opera House
c. 1899
Collection of John and Dorothy Kimiecik

In 1875, the building on the left, 16 South Main Street in Florida, was owned by Miss. J. Aspell. In 1903, it housed the Willet Vail Opera House. At that time it was one of the few amusement places in the village and soon became a great success.

Florida Grocery Store
c. 1930
Florida Historical Society

The building above shown under construction and shown at left finished, seems to have been used initially as a grocery store when corn was 12¢ a can, soap was 4 for 25¢ and Jello was 10¢. It expanded into general merchandise as Clarence DeKay's 3¢ to 49¢ Store, as shown in the photo below.

DeKay's Store
c. 1925
Reprinted from Florida Historical book [2]

In the 1920s, Willet Vail's Opera House later became Clarence DeKay's "The Christmas Store."

The Historical Society of the Town of Warwick

A. H. Drew Store
c. 1903
Historical Society of the Town of Warwick

In 1903, the A. H. Drew store was at the corner of McEwen and Main streets in Warwick (where Yesterday's restaurant is today.)

Warwick A & P Store
c. 1920
Collection of the A & P Historical Society

By the 1920s, the wooden store pictured above was gone and the corner store was now the Warwick A & P.

Warwick A & P Store Interior
c. 1915-1920
Historical Society of the Town of Warwick, Joslyn Collection

The Warwick A & P store was at the corner of McEwen and Main Street, on the south side of the intersection. A can of Bell's poultry seasoning was 8 cents, and coffee was 24 cents a pound.

Closeup of A & P logo.

137

Days Gone By   A History in Pictures Town of Warwick, New York 1827-1945

Hazen's Store Minard Hazen built his store in 1887, on the northwest corner of
c. 1910 Windermere Avenue and Waterstone Road in Greenwood Lake.[40]
Collection of Taylor and Parker

Raynor's Market The store was later bought by Fred Cary Raynor, and converted to
c. 1930 house several separate stores. Fred Cary Raynor in center doorway,
Collection of Bill Raynor right. The man on the left of Raynor is probably store manager John
Sleigh, a philatelist and a main instigator of the Rocket Mail project
(see Celebrations section for more information on Rocket Mail).

H. D. House Store
c. 1910
Historical Society of the Town of Warwick, Joslyn Collection

The H. D. House store on Railroad Avenue in Warwick sold fruits, vegetables, candy, and baked goods—the perfect "pick up" store on the way home from the train.

Enlargements of above photo show details of clothing and store front. In days gone by, getting home delivery of your groceries was a service that all stores offered. Imagine that!

Soda Fountain
c. 1910
Historical Society of the Town of Warwick, Joslyn Collection

Soda fountain interior was likely on Main Street in Warwick. Until the 1960s, it was common for both small town and big city dwellers to enjoy carbonated beverages at local soda fountains and ice cream saloons. Often housed together with a pharmacy, the soda fountain counter served as a meeting place for people of all ages. However, the popularity of soda fountains declined with the introduction of fast foods, commercial ice cream, and bottled soft drinks.

Raynor's Market
c. 1940s
Photographed by Roy Elston, Collection of Bill Raynor

Photo shows Raynor's Market on Main Street in Warwick, with a 1936 delivery truck in front. Raynor's Market is probably the oldest surviving business on Main Street. Founded by Fred Cary Raynor originally on McEwen Street, they specialized in homemade sausage.

Interior of Local Store
c. 1930
Photographed by Kinney
Collection of the Simms Family

Edenville Store
c. 1930s
Collection of Warwick United Methodist Church, Gift of Hazel Miller

The Edenville Store is now Country Dream Restaurant. Shown is owner Seely Everett and his family.

M. M. Rounsavell Store, Main Street, Warwick
c. 1915
Historical Society of the Town of Warwick

Trusdell Store
In 1903 the Trusdell Store was owned by L. G. Trusdell who was a local petit juror in 1890.

Warwick Valley Telephone
1907
Historical Society of the Town of Warwick, Advertiser Supplement 1907

Telephone operator in the "new" Warwick Valley Telephone building—the Finch Building on Main Street. The third floor housed the offices and the other two stories were leased out. In 1907, there were 315 phones installed, going as far as Pine Island and Vernon.

Stidworthy's Garage, South Street, Opposite Railroad Avenue
c. 1938
Collection of Jon Stidworthy

Warwick Auto Company
c. 1940s
Collection of Gary Randall

The Warwick Auto Company was on Railroad Avenue. Car at pumps is a 1934 Pontiac two-door "bustle back" touring sedan. This new model sold for $745 and featured a built-in trunk.

First National Bank
c. 1910
Historical Society of the Town of Warwick

The First National Bank in Warwick was organized in 1864, and was located in the brick building at the corner of West and Main. By 1907 it had built its own building at Bank and Main streets.

First National Bank Interior
c. 1907
Historical Society of the Town of Warwick

The First National Bank in Warwick on opening day of the new building. Shown (we assume from left to right) are Fred Wood, Fred Cary, Charles A. Crissey in background, Rensallaer Demarest, and Joseph Sayre.

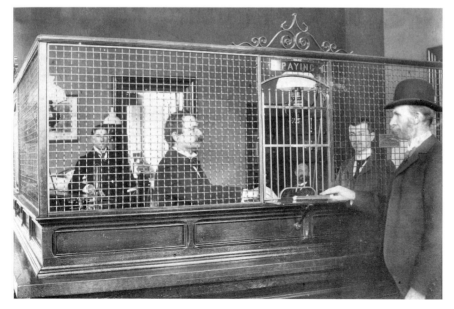

Celebrations & Events

Forester Square
c. 1920
Historical Society of the Town of Warwick

Forester Square, at the corner of Colonial Avenue and Main Street Warwick. The corner park created by the Sanford Memorial Fountain and Bandstand was the site of many festive celebrations over the years.

At the Hoo Doo Parade, a "maypole dance" on Main Street was part of the festivities to welcome Spring. The pole is in front of the Charles W. Lewis home, also owned by the Cowdrey family and later taken down. An earlier version of the bandstand is shown, as well as the Dr. Cary house (just to left of peak of gazebo), which was taken down in 1886. Photo appears to be taken from an upper floor or roof of the United States Hotel, which stood where the present-day Mobil station is. At left is the small house, one of the oldest in the village, which was torn down and the Albert Wisner Library built on its site.

Hoo Doo Parade in Warwick
May 6, 1885
Historical Society of the Town of Warwick

The Historical Society of the Town of Warwick

Main Street Parade in Warwick
c. 1865-1870s
Historical Society of the Town of Warwick

This stereoscope image shows a parade on Main Street in Warwick, but we do not know what the celebration was. Note third floor on building at right, which was removed in the early decades of the 20th century.

Main Street Parade in Warwick
c. 1920
Historical Society of the Town of Warwick

Another parade on Main Street in Warwick. Although African Americans and other minorities were part of Warwick's community from its earliest days, photographs that include them are less common—the majority of surviving photos are formal portraits which were usually of the well-to-do white families.

Main Street Parade in Florida
c. 1900
Photographed by James Razey
Florida Historical Society

Taken during a parade in front of the Fire House on South Main Street in Florida.

Main Street Gathering in Florida
1899
Florida Historical Society

The photograph above was taken outside the Aspell House, 32 North Main Street in Florida, during either a horse auction or a Christmas celebration.

Civil War

From the History of Forester Square by Hylah Hasbrouck

In 1862 when Warwick sent its quota of men to the 124th regiment they started from the old Wawayanda Hotel. On the day of departure, they lined up in front, Captain Benedict at their head, and were given flags which a group of ladies including Mrs. Clara Edsall and Mrs. Grinnell Burt had raised the money for and bought. One of these flags is in Washington's headquarters in Newburgh and the other is in the capitol at Albany.

Orange Blossoms Reunion
c. 1897
Collection of the Beattie, Jacob, and May Family

Veterans of the Civil War, the 124th NYS Volunteers, or "Orange Blossoms," at a reunion in Gettysburg.[41]

Grand Army of the Republic Reunion
c. 1900-1915
Historical Society of the Town of Warwick

The 124th Regiment of the Grand Army of the Republic (G.A.R.), local Civil War veterans, gathered at their monument in Goshen.

Below: Warwick G.A.R. Reunion
c. 1885-1900
Historical Society of the Town of Warwick

Reunion of the Warwick G.A.R., showing in front row, left to right: General Ward, Capt. James W. Benedict, Dominy Litchfield, Capt. J. Wood Houston. The location is noted as probably in Servin's field, which would be in the vicinity of Memorial Park.

World War I Homecoming
c. 1918
Historical Society of the Town of Warwick
(for following photos until next credit line)

Warwick welcomes its World War I veterans home with a parade, including musical accompaniment on homemade instruments…

…and hanging the Kaiser in effigy, a way of seeking closure after enduring a long, horrible war; we would probably not feel comfortable with this type of expression today!

Presentation of the troops, which included women who served as well, in front of Village Hall.

The Parade ended at the Old School Baptist Meeting House, with fine speeches.

The Old School Baptists were quite strict, but actually enjoyed much more comfortable winter church-going conditions than the current community, which experiences Christmas Eve services in an unheated church. There once were coal stoves on each side, as

evidenced by the chimneys in this picture, but these were removed when the church was restored by the Historical Society, for the safety of the building.

Community Chautauqua
c. 1904-1910
Historical Society of the Town of Warwick, Joslyn Collection

The "Chautauqua" movement started in 1874 in its name place in NY. Circuit Chautauquas were traveling tent shows starting in 1904 that combined adult education with morally uplifting content. Here we see a location most likely somewhere in the Village of Warwick. We see new sidewalks, fire hydrants, and the young maple trees that were planted around the turn of the century under Clinton Wheeler Wisner.

Clam Bake
c. 1910
Historical Society of the Town of Warwick

Near the Wawayanda House, along Forester Avenue, was a patch of woods owned by the Servin family (called "Servin's Woods") where many community events were held, such as this clam bake. The dapper gentlemen in the front row, third from the left, is Mayor Clinton Wheeler Wisner.

Onion Harvest Festival 1939

Held in mid-August at different intervals from 1939-1999, the festival was filled with the pageantry of Old World costumes, music, and such national dances as the polonaise, mazur, and oberek, as well as many regional dances. More than 200 area residents from five years of age to adult danced in the 1999 festival.

The event recreates the traditional Polish ceremonial *dozynki*, or harvest celebration, before the symbolic *panatwo gosdodarze*, or lord and lady of the manor. The first festival in Warwick was held in 1939, organized by a committee with members from the various Black Dirt communities. Father Raith of Florida was the chairperson (efforts to begin the festival one year earlier were stymied by a devastating flood in 1938, which wrought ruin on the crops). It was held on the Albert Durland Farm, just over the border in Goshen.

The format for the traditional festival is that the day begins with Holy Mass which may be held outdoors. The harvesters (peasants) are decked out in their regional finery. Someone represents the *dziedzic* (squire, lord, nobleman) and his family. During the offering, in addition to communion wafers and wine, harvesters bring the harvest wreath, other herbs, sheaves of grain, baskets of fruit, and other crops symbolizing the abundance of the harvest.

The harvesters slowly process to the "lord." As they go, they sing typical, merry harvest songs, one of which runs as follows:

Carry harvest's yield, to squire from the field.
May the harvest give its bounty
Biggest crop yields in the county,
Carry harvest's yield.

The *przodownica* or best girl harvester wears the harvest wreath as a kind of headpiece. It is made of woven golden grain, decorated with meadow flowers, with small apples or clusters of mountain-ash berries and often beribboned for added color. She presents the wreath to the "squire" who hangs it up in a place of honor in his home. He then pours himself and the oldest male harvester a glass of vodka and toasts the entire company.

After the meal, the "squire" dances the first dance with the *przodownica*, and his wife dances with the *przodownik* (leading male harvester). Afterward all are invited to join in. In a Polish American setting, the *dozynki* usually features a folk-dance performance.

Onion Harvest Festival Queen
1939
Reprinted from the Onion Harvest Festival Book, 1989

The Onion Harvest Festival Queen in 1939 was Martha Plock of Florida.

Eleanor Roosevelt Adresses Festival
1939
Photo by Msgr. John S. Felczak

Collection of Barbara Morgiewicz

First Lady Eleanor Roosevelt addresses the crowd at the 1939 Onion Harvest Festival. She also lunched with Ms. Florence Ketchum, the editor of the *Warwick Dispatch*. Due to their proximity to Warwick while at Hyde Park, Mrs. Roosevelt took an interest in Warwick's doings on several occasions. She visited the NYS Training School for Boys in June 1945, and also intervened on one occasion when the local currant crop was rejected for market.

Children Dancing at Festival
1939
Reprinted from the Onion Harvest Festival Book, 1989

Children dance the "Zasily Farmerzy Cebule."

Greenwood Lake Rocket Mail
February 1936

In February of 1936, a group of stamp collecting enthusiasts partnered with the Rocket Airplane Corporation of America, headed up by the scientist Willy Ley. They would use a rocket engine on a small airplane to send mail across the state line at Greenwood Lake. Fred W. Kessler, a prominent member of the American Air Mail Society, arranged for special postcards to be loaded on the plane. Each was imprinted with "Via First American-Rocket Airplane Flight" and had a red rocket stamp which cost 50 cents.

On Febuary 9, the first rocket was prepared on the New York side shore, near Morningside County Club. Mounted on a catapult and headed toward the Hewitt side of the lake, it was christened the "Gloria" by six-year-old Gloria Sleigh, daughter of local philatelist John Sleigh. The temperature was not right for the liquid oxygen and hydrogen fuel; an alternate rocket was prepared, and ignited. It fizzed and hissed but went nowhere—the cable release on the catapult had frozen. As the day waned, the second attempt was made, but the glider moved sluggishly up the ramp and hung there. It seems this time they had forgotten to release the cable on the catapult!

The crowd reassembled for another attempt two weeks later on February 23. More than 700 people, who had walked more than a mile from where their cars were parked, waited nearly six hours in the frigid air. This time, with the help of smooth ice, one of the rockets became airborne and slid across the state line—a flight totalling about 2,000 feet. The mail was promptly taken to the post office by Hewitt postmaster Walter White for distribution.

The stills below were extracted from film confiscated in Germany at the end of World War II. It is of the initial failed flights, and the German text made no mention of a later successful flight, but highlighted the incompetence of the Americans. It is interesting to note that Mr. Kessler, after the second successful flight, swore out a warrant for an unnamed mechanic whom he charged with malicious mischief and blamed for the previous failures.[42]

Greenwood Lake Rocket Mail Movie
February 1936
Historical Society of the Town of Warwick

The rocket is loaded on the ramp....

Conditions for ignition of the fuel are checked.   The ship is christened "Gloria."   The crowd waits anxiously in the worsening weather.   Ignition!

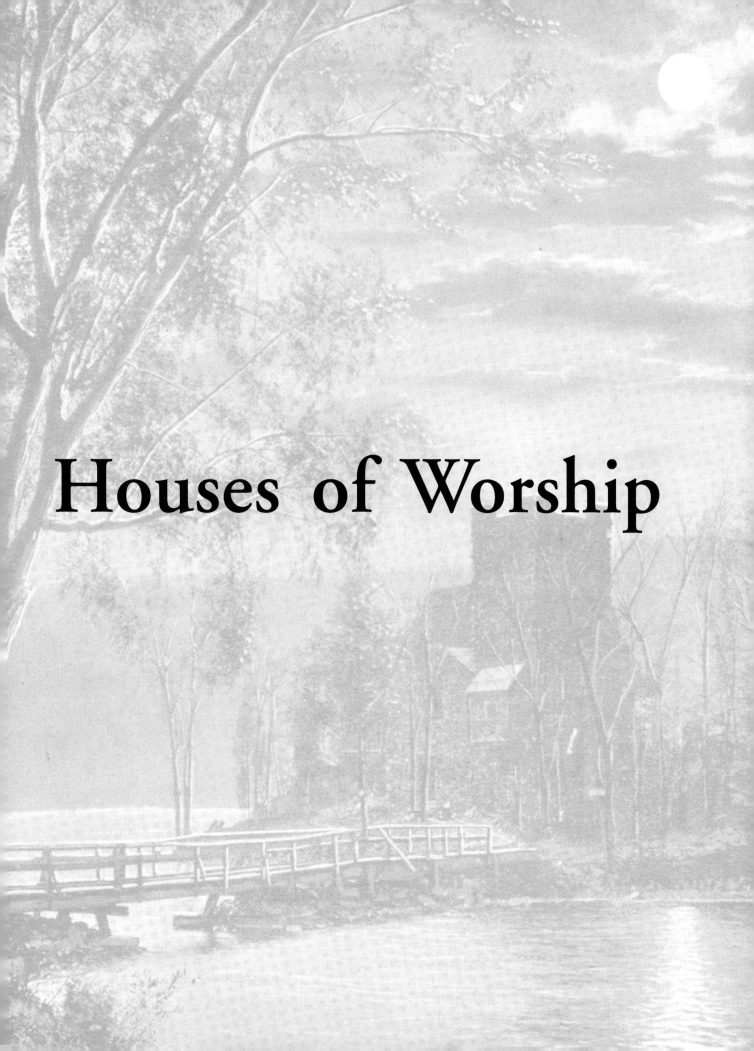

Houses of Worship

Vespers Service
The Free Church of Strangers
Chapel Island, Greenwood Lake
c. 1900
Collection of Nina Steen

There is probably no more picturesque a scene in Warwick's history than the church that stood in Greenwood Lake. The church was the result of the never-ending quest of Satella Sharps Waterstone and other community leaders to establish a church here. After years of services at her home, Waterstone Cottage, her dream was finally realized, and in 1885, a tent was erected on what then called Limerock Island. A structure gradually grew, and in 1902, when it became part of the newly incorporated *Church of The Good Shepherd*, a tower was built. In July and August, services were held on Chapel Island. People arrived by rowboat, canoe, or in later years, motorboats. The calm of the lake, the voices of the choir drifting over the water, and the peacefulness that prevailed made for an experience that few could forget. The last service was held on Dec. 17, 1944, and four years later the landmark was destroyed by fire.

Chapel Island by Moonlight
c. 1910
Collection of Nina Steen

Chapel Island
1913
Historical Society of the Town of Warwick

Good Shepherd Parish Greenwood Lake
c. 1915-1930
Collection of Nina Steen

The Episcopal Church of the Good Shepherd Greenwood Lake parish house was built in 1910, on land donated by Mr. and Mrs. Solomon Caldwell. For many years, summer services were held at Chapel Island. Severely damaged by fire in December 1943, the parish house was repaired, renovated, and in 1954, a new tower was added to house the Chapel Island bell.

Interior, Church of the Good Shepherd
Christmas, 1922
Collection of Church of the Good Shepherd

As with most churches, the interior was remodeled several times.

Holy Rosary Church Greenwood Lake
c. 1927-1935
Collection of Nina Steen

Holy Rosary Church in Greenwood Lake was built in 1927 as a mission church of St. Stephen's in Warwick. Before this church was built, Catholics attended Our Lady of the Lake in Sterling Forest or St. Stephen's. Holy Rosary was made a parish in 1954. The adjoining rectory was built in 1958.

Bellvale Methodist Church
c. 1940s
Collection of E. Roecker

A Methodist class was organized at Bellvale in 1809. A church was built in 1853. The original church burned to the ground in January 1940. By July 18 of the same year, the cornerstone was laid for this new structure.[43]

Amity Presbyterian First Church
c. 1800
Collection of Estella Youngman

The first church began in 1797 and was finished in 1800. The second church (at right) was erected in 1828. The third church (below) was erected in 1868. This is the present-day church, which was remodeled from 1930-1931 (bottom right).

Amity Presbyterian Second Church
c. 1828
Collection of Estella Youngman

Amity Presbyterian Third Church
c. 1868
Collection of Estella Youngman

Amity Presbyterian Church Remodeling
c. 1931
Collection of Estella Youngman

The Historical Society of the Town of Warwick

St. Stephen's Church Interior
c. 1910
Historical Society of the Town of Warwick, Joslyn Collection

Worship styles change over the years, too. The interiors of many Roman Catholic Churches changed dramatically after the 1960s.

The church at the corner of Second and South Streets is now home of the Warwick Assembly of God.

St. Stephen's Second Church
c. 1904
Historical Society of the Town of Warwick

The first church was a small chapel on Church Street in Warwick, this new structure on South Street replaced it.

Warwick's Christ Episcopal Church
c. 1870
Collection of Christ Church

The church was finished in December of 1866. The American Gothic structure was designed by Mr. Jardine and built by Henry McElroy. The cost, including the lot and interior, was around $9,000.

Christ Episcopal Church Interior
c. 1910-1915
Historical Society of the Town of Warwick, Joslyn Collection

Days Gone By   A History in Pictures Town of Warwick, New York 1827-1945

Christ Episcopal Church Celebration
1942
Collection of Christ Church

The Rev. Wickersham II was instituted as Rector and posed with the choir, altar boys, and others that participated in the liturgy.

Old School Baptist Meeting House
Before 1915
Historical Society of the Town of Warwick

The Old School Baptist Meeting House was built in 1810 when the Baptist congregation founded in 1765 outgrew the original meeting house at the corner of Galloway Road (17A) and Forester Avenues. Designed by John Morris Foght with interior details and carpentry by Azariah Ketchum, the church incorporated unusual details for the time period, such as Gothic arch windows and a wineglass pulpit. The pulpit that stands there today is a reproduction, based on a similar pulpit still existing at the Slate Hill church. It is unusual to see a group of children like this at the church, as one of the differences between "Old School" and "New School" Baptists was that the original congregation did not approve of Sunday School—asserting that religious education should not be relegated to one day a week, but continuous and in the context of the family. The congregation gradually diminished, the church deteriorated, and the church was scheduled for demolition by the State, but was rescued by the Historical Society under the leadership of Mrs. Madison Lewis in 1952.

Calvary Baptist Church
c. 1918-1925
Historical Society of the Town of Warwick

Calvary Baptist Church, located on West Street in Warwick, was founded in 1865, following differences in the Baptist congregation. This church on West Street was completed in 1868.

158

Moving Warwick's Reformed Church
c. 1890
Historical Society of the Town of Warwick

Warwick Reformed Church was built in 1847-1848. Churches are not immune to the winds of change, and when the congregation determined to build the present stone church (completed in this view, see mid left of photo), the old one was moved down the street, and is now Village Hall. Would we attempt this today? Harvey McPeek, moving engineer extraodinaire, took up the challenge and said he could move it intact—and he did, with the help of friends, neighbors, a few horses, log rollers, and a windlass![44]

Methodist Episcopal Church
c. 1915
Historical Society of the Town of Warwick

The Warwick Methodist Episcopal church on Main Street in Warwick was built in 1865. Repeated lightning strikes to the steeple caused much damage over the years. When it was damaged again in 1918, the crenallated tower that we know today as the "Clock Tower" replaced the steeple. The clock was installed in 1907, a gift to the Village from Pierson Ezra Sanford.

Replacing Steeple
c. 1918
Historical Society of the Town of Warwick

The Warwick Methodist Episcopal Church has its damaged steeple removed, and the new crenellated tower created.

Clock Tower
c. 1919
Historical Society of the Town of Warwick

The house that stood next to what is now known as the Clock Tower Building stood where the current CVS parking lot is. A story is told that when the clock was first installed, several people who did not know it had been started ran out into the street in a panic the first time it struck, thinking it was the fire alarm.

New Milford Methodist Church
1938
From the Warwick Valley Dispatch, 9/28/1938

In 1789, the congregation first met in the home of Cornelius Lazear, whose home was also a tavern. His place was nicknamed the "Methodist Tavern." The New Milford Methodist Church was organized and land bought in 1838. This photo was taken during the centennial celebration of the church building.

The Historical Society of the Town of Warwick

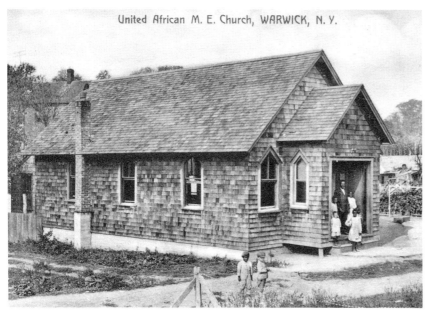

United African Methodist Church in Warwick
c. 1910
Historical Society of the Town of Warwick

The United African Methodist Church in Warwick has stood on McEwen Street for 100 years. It is planned to be removed in the near future to make way for a new home for the congregation.

Convent at Mount Alverno
c. 1920
Collection of Barbara Morgiewicz

The convent at Mt. Alverno housed the novitiate of the order since early in its history.

Aerial view of Mt. Alverno
Grand Street, Warwick
c. 1930
Collection of Nina Steen

St. Stanislaus R. C. Church
Pine Island
c. 1915
Collection of Barbara Morgiewicz

The St. Stanislaus Roman Catholic Church in Pine Island was founded in 1912, after a group of forty Polish families petitioned for establishment of a parish. The church is named after the patron Saint of Poland who was the Bishop of Krakow. The first priest was Stanislaus J. Nowak.

Presbyterian Church
Florida
c. 1900
Reprinted from Florida Historical book [2]

The roots of the Presbyterian Church in Florida date back to 1742 when the "Men of Brookland" built a meeting house for worship. Following a fire in 1837, this church edifice was built and dedicated in June of 1838.

St. Joseph's Roman Catholic Parish
Florida
c. 1930
From the collection of John and Dorothy Kimiecik

St. Joseph's Roman Catholic Parish, 18 Glenmere Avenue in Florida, was built in 1895. Following the Civil War, large scale European migration to the United States began. Many difficulties faced the early Polish immigrants, the language barrier being at the top of the list. For these deeply religious people a priest who spoke their language was essential. After many years of traveling to other parishes, local Polish people were ecstatic when Father Nowak, born in Poland, arrived in Florida in 1895, to oversee the construction of the church pictured at left.

Father Raith of St. Joseph
c. 1930
Reprinted from Florida Historical book [2]

Father Raith, pictured driving the car, was instrumental in transforming St. Joseph's Cemetery in Florida into the "lawn plan" in 1936. Notice the car's acetylene lamps and klaxon horn—a very expensive vehicle!

**St. Edward's Roman Catholic Church
Florida
c. 1900**
Florida Historical Society

St. Edward's Roman Catholic Church, built in 1844 on North Main Street in Florida, originally housed the "second" Presbyterian Church of Florida. Divisions in the Presbyterian congregation caused the dissident group to break away and form a second church until they returned to the original congregation early in 1887. Due to an increase in the Catholic population in Florida and the surrounding area, in June 1887 the parish of St. Stephen's Roman Catholic Church in Warwick purchased the building and established the mission church of St. Edward's. It was officially incorporated in February 1889.

**St. Joseph's Father Nowak
c. 1899**
Reprinted from Florida Historical book [2]

Monsignor Stanislaus J. Nowak came from Poland in 1895 to oversee the construction of St. Joseph's Roman Catholic Parish in Florida, NY.

**Methodist Episcopal
Church in Florida
c. 1905**
Collection of Dr. Richard Hull

The Florida Methodist Episcopal Church was built c. 1837 on South Main Street. The church had its origin in the wagon-making shop of Justus Dill. By 1881 the size of the congregation declined, the church was disbanded and the building was sold to John Weed; it became known as Weed's Hall. The building has served the community as a movie house, play house, and assembly hall.

Temple Beth Shalom
Roosevelt Avenue, Florida
c. 1951
Collection of Temple Beth Shalom

Jewish immigrants had been arriving in the area since the 19th century, often settling near Florida to be among the Polish Catholics they had known in the old country. Later on, Greenwood Lake became a center for summer residences for those of Jewish heritage coming from New York's Lower East Side. This congregation was formed in 1947 as the Hebrew Community Center. The congregation's building pictured above was built in 1951. The Hebrew Community Center was renamed Temple Beth Shalom in the early 1960s to better reflect its role as a house of worship.

Daily Life

Days Gone By   A History in Pictures Town of Warwick, New York 1827-1945

View from Red Swan Inn
c. 1915
Historical Society of the Town of Warwick

The view from the Red Swan Inn across Route 94 at the intersection of 17A (Galloway Road) was much more bucolic nearly a century ago.

The Willows
c. 1915
Historical Society of the Town of Warwick

Forester Avenue, lined with Willow trees, in the Village of Warwick, was just a dirt track called "Burt's Lane" 150 years or so ago. Then the road became known as "Lake Street" because it led past a pool of the Wawayanda. Up until the mid 20th century it was still unpaved and ran through the Servin farm.

Wawayanda Creek Crossing
c. 1915
Historical Society of the Town of Warwick

Photo shows Wawayanda Creek crossing, possibly at Forester Avenue or Pelton Road (Route 1). We tend to romanticize days gone by, and think of scenes like these boys enjoying a long summer afternoon at the creek.

Picking Daisies
c. 1915
Historical Society of the Town of Warwick, Joslyn Collection

Who could resist taking time to pick a bouquet of daisies, perhaps to while away some hours making daisy chains, when an entire field-full beckoned?

Making A Basket
c. 1920
Photo by G. A. Williams
Collection of Beattie, Jacob, and May Family

Warwickians of the past spent most of their days just as we do today, in the enterprise of making a living. Here a member of the Conklin family, most likely Webb, making a basket. This family was noted for many years for their excellent handmade baskets.

Rag Carpet Weaving Bellvale
c. 1901-1915
Historical Society of the Town of Warwick, Frangos Collection

Viner Shawcross weaving rag rugs in Bellvale. Textiles were produced by hand for a long time. Often people would save their rags and then take them to be cut up and woven into rugs.

Renovating A Grape Arbor
c. 1900-1926
Historical Society of the Town of Warwick, Joslyn Collection

Photo shows gardener renovating a grape arbor. He appears to be on the F. C. Cary property on Main Street in Warwick, about where the current post office stands. Over his shoulder on the left is the house that stood where the Albert Wisner Library is; to the right is the Wawayanda House hotel. This photo dates from before the road was cut down to elminate a hill, as the basement level of the hotel is still below ground.

Gardener
c. 1900-1926
Historical Society of the Town of Warwick, Joslyn Collection

The gardener takes a break, posing with his wheel barrow.

Sharpening Tools
c. 1915-1920
Historical Society of the Town of Warwick Gift of Alice Foley Martin

They had an axe to grind! Members of a Warwick family at their summer home on Wawayanda Lake sharpen tools on a hand-cranked grinding wheel.

Mill Crew
c. 1915-1920
Historical Society of the Town of Warwick, Gift of Alice Foley Martin

In this photo, the mill crew takes a short break. Local saw mills played a great part in the history of the Town. In the days before lumber was transported long distances by truck and rail to Warwick, most building materials for Warwick were gathered from our own woods. In 1839, New York was the leader in timber production, accounting for 30 percent of all lumber produced. By 1854 in Orange County alone there were 36 saw mills. Nineteenth-century mills used either water or steam power, and were often temporary structures.[45]

Delivering Lumber
c. 1912
Historical Society of the Town of Warwick, Gift of Alice Foley Martin

The team driver delivers a load of lumber to a happy customer. Wood use changed our landscape dramatically. In earlier times, the iron industry and wood needed for heat decimated the forests to the point where by the mid 1800s citizens wondered what the future would hold, when all the woods were gone. Everyone who could afford to owned a wood lot just so they could have access to this resource.

Grading the Road
c. 1910
Collection of Barbara Morgiewicz

Photo shows a horse-drawn road grader which would scrape the road surface smooth again. This had to be done periodically to dirt roads, which were churned up by wagon wheels and hoofs.

Days Gone By   A History in Pictures Town of Warwick, New York 1827-1945

Heading Out to Field
c. 1890-1910
Collection of Bill Raynor

Much of the typical day for many of our citizens in the early years was in growing and caring for crops and livestock. Here a wagon designed for heavy loads, with extra wide wheels to avoid bogging down, heads out to the field. This is the Raynor Farm at Hathorn Road and Route 94. The house in the background stood in the field in front of the Chateau Hathorn.

Tending the Family Garden
c. 1912
Shulman Family Scrapbook
Gift of Herbert Shulman

Isaac Shulman and his son Fred in the garden, on Wheeler Avenue in Warwick. Most families of the past had a family garden from which they harvested fresh vegetables, and canned extra produce for the winter. Isaac immigrated here from Russia around 1858.

Below: "Make hay while the sun shines" meant that in order to make sure the livestock was fed through the winter, hay had to be cut, allowed to dry, and stacked or baled before rainfall rotted and ruined it. Often all hands had to pitch in. Even for those who were well-to-do, manual labor was a necessary part of life.

Making Hay
c. 1912
Collection of Beattie, Jacob, and May Family

Here Don Wilder (on ground), of the Victor Audubon Wilder estate (now the Chateau Hathorn), works the fields. Oxen were often used for hauling the heaviest loads.

Houston Homestead
Edenville
c. 1930s
*Collection of John and Virginia Clancey
(for all photos on this page)*

Mr. and Mrs. Joseph Houston pose on the lawn of their Edenville farm. The house is on the corner of present-day Pine Island Turnpike (barn and haywagon are across the street) and the present-day County Route 1.

Below: A load of hay comes in to the Houston homestead. Notice the triangular pole structure which was found on most farms, and is called a "gin pole." This sturdily anchored and braced pole, usually with a pulley system at the top, would be used to lift and move heavy loads. In the days before hay balers, sometimes the haystack would be piled right around the pole (bottom photo).

Onion Farming in the Black Dirt Region
c. 1940s
Photo by Msgr. John S. Felczak
Collection of Barbara Morgiewicz

The famous Black Dirt agricultural region has existed for less than 150 years. Once an enormous water meadow and swamp, it was gradually drained in a series of projects spurred by the arrival of Polish and German-Russian immigrants who saw opportunity in its rich black loam. Prior to this, farmers used the meadows for grazing.

For Black Dirt families, getting the onion crop in meant weeks of hand-pulling the onions to dry.

Hand-Sorting Onions
c. 1940s
Photo by Msgr. John S. Felczak
Collection of Barbara Morgiewicz

Harvesting Onions
c. 1940s
Photo by Msgr. John S. Felczak
Collection of Barbara Morgiewicz

Everyone pitched in to get the crop harvested. In the early years, it was the Polish and German families who harvested the crops. Later on, as farms expanded and family size decreased, migrant workers from Mexico and Central America began to appear to help during the growing season and harvest.

Laying Water Pipe
c. 1900-1915
Historical Society of the Town of Warwick

Water was brought to the Village of Warwick in 1871 and a great celebration was held on January 10, 1872—the "Mistucky Water Celebration." A second Village reservoir was built in 1891. New pipe for the system was laid in 1903, when the old began to deteriorate. This image came from a local glass plate negative collection, but we've been unable to verify that this was part of Warwick's water system being constructed.

Horse-Driven Thresher
Before 1915
Historical Society of the Town of Warwick

Horse-driven machinery was a necessity. At right is a crew threshing buckwheat. Horse-driven threshers were in use by the early 1800s. The owner of the machine and a work team would usually travel around and hire out their services. It took a team of several men to keep up with feeding the machine and bagging the grain.

Horse-Driven Machine
c. 1915
Collection of Barbara Morgiewicz

We've been unable to determine the use of the mystery machine at left.

Horse-Drawn Sled
1915
Historical Society of the Town of Warwick
Shulman Family Scrapbook

Fred and Alice Shulman with their horse "Dixie." Horses were essential for transportation as well as work.

173

Horse-Drawn Wagon
1900
Historical Society of the Town of Warwick Shulman Family Scrapbook

Horses also made the wheels of business go round. Merchants often would sell from wagons that traveled the back roads. Max and Isaac Shulman, Russian immigrants, started out walking from farm to farm with their goods in packs. Eventually they acquired their dry goods store, originally on Railroad Avenue. Later they moved up to Main Street into the building which is now Newhard's. It was also the home of Gilvan's for many years.

Delivering Ice
c. 1915
Historical Society of the Town of Warwick, Joslyn Collection

The ice man comes! Before electricity gave us modern refrigeration, "ice boxes" were how people kept their food fresh. This delivery man is in Warwick at the corner of Railroad Avenue and South Street.

Local Markets
c. 1940s
Photo possibly by Roy Elston Courtesy of Richard Hull

Still a common sight today, local growers marketed locally as well as shipping their produce to bigger markets. A load of potatoes and a sunny day helped pay the bills.

Searsmobile
1928
Historical Society of the Town of Warwick

Martin Van Buren Horton in his 1910 Searsmobile on Main Street in Warwick in front of the Miller Building, when it was the home of the Warwick Savings Bank. Searsmobiles were also called "High Wheelers" as they could go anywhere a wagon could go because of the large wheels and high clearance. He owned a sawmill and enjoyed touring around in his vintage auto. It didn't have much power and local boys were known to pitch in and help him out by pushing it up a steep hill.[46]

Commuting to NYC
c. 1932-1939
Collection of Motor Bus Society, Courtesy of Wade Bates

The commute into "The City" has been a part of life for Warwick residents ever since the railroad first made quicker travel possible. The Warwick Stage Line operated for many years, running to the 50th Street Grayhound terminal until the late 1950s, when it was switched to Port Authority. This is a 1932 bus model, in the 1930s at the 50th Street station.

Warwick Express
c. 1941
Collection of Motor Bus Society, Courtesy of Wade Bates

Here we see a 1941 model, which seated 33 people.

Harvesting Ice in the Black Dirt Region
c. 1932-1939
Collection of Barbara Morgiewicz

There was no such thing as "down time" for black dirt farm families. In the winter, the crop of choice was ice. Here a family waits to unload at the Pine Island Creamery.

Blizzard of 1888, Warwick Main St.
1888
Historical Society of the Town of Warwick

Extreme weather has always been one of life's challenges for residents of the valley. The Blizzard of 1888 brought the Northeast to a standstill.

Snow Tunnel
c. 1913
Collection of Beattie, Jacob, and May Family

A "snow tunnel!" And we think we have problems with clearing the snow today! Horses and sleighs didn't need the street entirely clear, but more than a foot or so made for hard going.

Blizzard of 1888, View Down West Street, Warwick
1888
Historical Society of the Town of Warwick

The Historical Society of the Town of Warwick

Flood of 1896, Warwick
1896
Historical Society of the Town of Warwick

If it wasn't snowstorms, it was rain. February 8, 1896, is written on the penant at top—that's the only way we know the date of this image of the regularly occurring floods of the Wawayanda. Location is South Street in Warwick. Notice the old railroad station is on the right.

Flood of 1896, Warwick
1896
Historical Society of the Town of Warwick

Another view of the Flood of 1896, looking north from the Main Street bridge in Warwick. The lower level of the shops on Main Street still flood occasionally—but not as bad as this!

Floods in the Black Dirt Region
c. 1940s
Photo by Msgr. John S. Felczak
Collection of Barbara Morgiewicz

Floods of biblical proportion are part of life in the black dirt. Despite many projects to control the flow of the Wallkill, over the years the water has claimed crops countless times. Not to be daunted, this farmer hand-carts his crop out of harm's way, and finds the humor to smile for the camera.

Days Gone By — A History in Pictures Town of Warwick, New York 1827-1945

A Mountain Family
c. 1915
Historical Society of the Town of Warwick
Gift of Alice Foley Martin

Just as today, not everyone in Warwick was well-to-do. Many lived back in the hills, and there was often a distinct class difference between the "villagers" and the more remote "mountaineers." Judging from the content of the album this was found in, this is likely in the area of Moe or Warwick Mountain.

Ethel Mabee and Daisy the Cow
c. 1915
Historical Society of the Town of Warwick
Gift of Alice Foley Martin

Rural families have always had special favorites among the livestock, and even named each of their cows. Young Ethel apparently had a great favorite in Daisy. You can just about hear her mom calling, "You stop fooling with that cow and come in and do your homework!"

Van Gelder's Family Pets & Hobbies
c. 1910
Historical Society of the Town of Warwick, Joslyn Collection

Below, the Van Gelder family poses with pets and hobbies evident. Apparently the younger daughter thought little of the plan. This is most likely the John VanGelder's, who lived on upper Main Street in Warwick about where Century 21 is today.

Wedding
c. 1920
Collection of Frances and Robert Sodrick

The wedding of Jess and Pauline Van Sickle of Pine Island—note the wedding shoes.

The Historical Society of the Town of Warwick

Lifestyles of the relatively rich and locally famous.
These images show typical interiors of the stately homes of Warwick.

An Interior at F. C. Cary House
September 1904
Historical Society of the Town of Warwick, Joslyn Collection

Dr. F. C. Cary's home stood on Main Street between Wheeler Avenue and Baird's Tavern, where Country Chevy is today. Previously owned by Joel B. Wheeler in 1875.

Room Interior, Unknown Location
c. 1915
Historical Society of the Town of Warwick, Joslyn Collection

An Interior at F. C. Cary House
September 1904
Historical Society of the Town of Warwick, Joslyn Collection

Another interior at the F. C. Cary house. Dr. Cary owned several properties, and was a physician.

Felix Villamil Family Interior Parlor, Florida
c. 1935
Collection of Suzanne Straton

The Felix Villamil Family assembled in their North Main Street Florida parlor for a photo by James Razey. Richard, Elena, Leonore (seated), Virginia (standing), Raymond, Mother Mary, Fernan, Father Felix Villamil.

Fishing
c. 1915
Collection of the Beattie, Jacob, and May Family

Not all of life in days gone by was work. Here we see Don Wilder fishing. Leisure pursuits included hiking, fishing, and getting together for picnics, much as we do today. The fishing in Warwick was so good that Fred E. Pond wrote an article in *American Angler*, July 1919, about the Warwick lakes.

Hiking
Before 1919
Warwick Valley Dispatch, April 19, 1919

Hiking the hills of this area has always been a popular pastime. Joel Henry Crissey (left), a friend of the famous naturalist John Burroughs (right), was an ardent observer of nature. They hiked together in Warwick upon occasion. Here they are shown overlooking Greenwood Lake. This photo was run with Crissey's death notice.[47]

Warwick Family Hiking on Local Mountain
c. 1915
Historical Society of the Town of Warwick, Gift of Alice Foley Martin

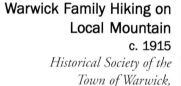

Making Ice Cream
c. 1915
Collection of the Beattie, Jacob, and May Family

Judge John J. Beattie (1849-1924) hand-cranking ice cream. He was a county court judge, and known throughout the region as an entertaining teller of tales and a great reader. His home is at the corner of Van Duzer Place and Maple Avenue in Warwick, and is still in the family.[48]

Building Stone Walls
1913
Collection of the Beattie, Jacob, and May Family

How did they move all those rocks? The miles of stone walls in Warwick were hauled and built by hand. To move stones and other heavy objects like root crops, a "stone boat" was used. This photo shows a hand-drawn variety, but usually horses were used to drag the load. The low profile meant you didn't have to lift things high to get them loaded. Here members of the Beattie family joke around for the camera.

A typical "stone boat." They were also called "drags."

Picking Fruit
1913
Collection of the Beattie, Jacob, and May Family

Shenanigans with an orchard ladder. Most families had at least a few fruit trees or an orchard, and tripod ladders like this are easier to prop up into the tree without breaking branches or knocking down the fruit. Today they are usually made of aluminum, but this one is a handmade antique.

Fun at the Lake
c. 1913
Collection of the Beattie, Jacob, and May Family

A rare view. Today a shot like this would be uncommon because most women don't grow their hair this long now, but this is an unusual view because in the early part of the 20th century women did not wear their hair down in public. They wore it in large buns, twists, and braids that were usually hidden under a hat when going out. To be photographed like this at the lake was either an act of youthful defiance or meant for "family viewing only."

The Family Orchard

Most family farms had an orchard for use by the household. The orchard would provide beauty in the spring when the blossoms appeared, and later in the year the crop would be harvested and the excess dried, canned, or sauces made. Methods of preserving fruit into the winter also included cold storage in "root cellars" underground. The phrase "it takes one bad apple to ruin the bunch" originated from this practice, for if a bruised fruit started to rot, it would hasten the decay of the rest of the fruit in the barrel.

Apple Picking
c. 1890
Florida Historical Society

Many days were spent apple picking on the farm of Charles W. Wheeler in Florida.

Relaxing
c. 1890
Florida Historical Society

Charles W. Wheeler and his son relaxing on the lawn of their farm in Florida.

Elizabeth W. Wheeler and Son
c. 1890
Florida Historical Society

The Historical Society of the Town of Warwick

Pony Ride
1906
Historical Society of the Town of Warwick, Joslyn Collection

The children or possibly the grandchildren of James Amherst Wisner enjoying a pony ride. By serendipity, we found that the pony cart was purchased from VanNess and delivered in the spring of 1906.[49]

A Bit of Historical Detective Work

Sometimes glass plate negative envelopes are mixed up or unlabeled so we must rely on clues in the pictures. The envelope of this glass plate negative was missing, but another envelope containing a similar picture said that they were the children of J. A. Wisner. This photo provided a valuable clue to the exact location: the elaborate greenhouses in the background.

Dunning Estate, Built 1856
1875
Atlas of Orange County, F. W. Beers

Sometimes, finding information on Warwick structures is like looking for a needle in a haystack, but on this one we got a lucky break—these greenhouses are also pictured in the engraving done in the 1875 Beers' *Atlas of Orange County*, on the estate of Benjamin F. Dunning. The Dunning Estate was located on Maple Avenue at what is now Pinecrest. Reportedly, these were the first greenhouses in Orange County. Mr. Dunning raised exotics like the Night Blooming Cereus, which blooms for only one night each year.

Wisner and Dunning, Neighbors
1903
Atlas of Orange County, J. M. Lathrop

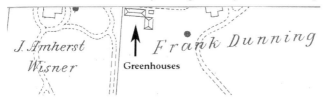

By looking at the map of Warwick in 1903, the map date closest to our photo, we can see that Wisner was indeed a neighbor of Dunning, and that the children were standing at the border of the Dunning property.

Out for a Ride
c. 1910
Collection of Don and Kathryn Lomax

Members of the Nanny family out for a ride. The Nannys owned what later became the Edenville Inn, on Waterbury Road.

Warwick Band to Appear on Radio Station WGNY
c. 1933-34
Collection of Bill Raynor

Radio station WGNY first operated out of the Golet Mansion on Golet Road near Glenmere. Here a Warwick band poses for a promotional photo. Shown are, L to R: Back row—Paul Wilkins, Charlie Bender, Bill Raynor; Front row—Frank Perna, Jim Edal, Harold Rudy.

The Oakland Theater, Warwick
1920
Historical Society of the Town of Warwick

The Oakland Theater in Warwick stood where the Burger King is today.

Education & Health

Days Gone By   A History in Pictures Town of Warwick, New York 1827-1945

"Common Schools" and The Public School System

As early as 1812, New York State organized a public school system. Long before this, however, "common schools" were funded by payment of tuition. There were many small schools dotted all over the Town. As populations increased and quicker transportation became available, the smaller schools were often folded into larger ones. In July 1926, Pine Island became the first Central School District in our town. In the 1950s, Warwick established a Central School District, which resulted in the closing of the neighborhood school houses. Some of them still survive as homes, but many are now gone.

New Milford School House
c. 1870-1875
Historical Society of the Town of Warwick

The school house at New Milford was typical of the many small district schools before centralization. It went through several transformations over the years. On the maps below, you can see that the school relocated across the road and northward sometime between 1859 and 1875.

1859 map by French and Beers   *1875 map by F. W. Beers*

Above we see the New Milford school house, possibly as it looked at the original location. This building may have been abandoned or burned; or possibly moved to the new location and extensively renovated. Fires were not uncommon in the days of wood heat; and the New Milford School did burn in the winter of 1921-22 and a new one was built.[50]

New Milford School House
c. 1875-1910
Historical Society of the Town of Warwick

New Milford School House
c. 1910
Historical Society of the Town of Warwick

New Milford School viewed from the south.

The Historical Society of the Town of Warwick

Ridge School
c. 1890-1900
Collection of Bill Raynor

The Ridge School was at the intersection of Ridge Road and Four Corners Road. The teacher is Lucy Smith Raynor.

A resident's memory of those early days in Warwick schools states that the preferred method of punishment was a switch about 2 rods long, also called a "rattan."

The Amity School
Date unknown
Historical Society of the Town of Warwick

The Amity School, prior to renovations of the 1970s.

St. Joseph's Polish School
Florida
1915
Collection of Barbara Morgiewicz

St. Peter's Evangelical Lutheran Church School
1926
Collection of St. Peter's Church

Parochial schools have played a part of Warwick's history since earliest times.

187

Bellvale School
c. 1910
Historical Society of the Town of Warwick

This brick building, although built in 1879, was not the first Bellvale School House. There were two earlier wooden ones which no longer exist. The former two were located very close to this brick one, but nearer to the road and smaller in size. Benjamin Burt sold the land to the Trustees for the first schoolhouse for $325.00 on May 1, 1826. There is no record as to what happened to the first building but a second wooden structure was built and used for many years. In a deed dated 1879, Andrew Houston sold an additional parcel of land for $200.00 for this brick building to be built.

Lake School
c. 1920
Collection of Marian Wright

Many people today do not realize that the hamlet of Lake, for which Lake Station Road was named, was a busy community with its own school.

Pine Island School Class
1925
Collection of Frances and Bob Sodrick

Frances Sodrick is in the front row, third from left.

Greenwood Lake Elementary School
c. 1927
Collection of Nina Steen

Greenwood Lake Elementary School; built in 1927, originally housed both the elementary and middle school for the Greenwood Lake school district. In 1961, an addition was built onto the west side of the building. Numbers of students increased so dramatically that in 1973, a separate Middle School had to be built on Lakes Road.

Washington Academy in Florida
Later, School No. 15
c. 1899

Florida Historical Society

The Washington Academy on North Main Street in Florida (c. 1806), began as a private school. William Henry Seward attended the Academy from 1811-1814. In 1812, it became a public school; the town was divided into school districts, and in 1813 the Academy became School No. 15 of the Town of Warwick.

The School on the Rock in Florida
School No. 2
c. 1900

Reprinted from Florida Historical book [2]

The School on the Rock, School No. 2 (c. 1800), was located at 30 Randall Street in Florida. William Henry Seward wrote that he received his first schooling here. The School on the Rock was a one-room schoolhouse built of stone and wood, complete with tales of witches living during the day in Roe's Woods above the school, and by night in the school's attic.

The Spanktown School House in Florida
School District No. 4
c. 1890

Reprinted from Florida Historical book [2]

The Spanktown School House (c. 1813) was located at the intersection of Spanktown Road and Union Corners Road in Florida. School District No. 4 was the educational starting-point for the children of many old, local families such as: Armstrong, Carr, Houston, Jessup, Pierson, Sly, and Wheeler. Today this building is being used for cemetery storage.

S. S. Seward Institute
c. 1890
Reprinted from Florida Historical book [2]

The first Florida S. S. Seward Institute building, formerly the Randolph Hotel, was a large three-story Greek Revival style structure (c. 1825). Opening in 1846, the Institute incorporated in 1847 and was accepted by the Board of Regents in 1848. Later, a sizeable two-story addition was built at the rear of the building for the growing student population.

Mt. Eve School
c. 1900
Collection of John and Dorothy Kimiecik

This class picture is from the Mt. Eve School District No. 3, one of Florida's one-room schoolhouses. The original 1833 school building was replaced in 1928 by another. Both buildings have survived, one as a private home.

Florida Schools
c. 1910
Reprinted from Florida Historical book [2]

This view of the Florida schools shows the later, 1893 brick school building built behind the first S. S. Seward Institute.

Seward Institute Women's Department
c. 1905
Reprinted from Florida Historical book [2]

In 1849, the Seward Institute Board of Trustees converted S. S. Seward's mansion into the Institute's female department. In 1910, ownership passed to Charles E. Packer and Charles Casterline, who renamed the building "Florida Lyceum," which featured live shows, dances, silent movies, and athletic contests.

S. S. Seward Institute Class Photo
c. 1923
Collection of John and Dorothy Kimiecik

The young lady circled in this class picture is Ann McBride. She graduated c. 1923, lived well into her nineties and was, for many years, the oldest living alumnae of S. S. Seward Institute.

Florida Public Schools Join Seward Institute
c. 1900
Collection of John and Dorothy Kimiecik

In 1893, this two-story brick school was built behind the Randolph Hotel building. That was when several Florida district schools and the Seward Institute were combined into one. When the building was expanded in 1929, the north and south walls of the original 1893 building were incorporated into the gym of the new school.

**The Warwick Institute
c. 1880s**
Historical Society of the Town of Warwick

A story is told that in the early years of the Institute, the boys would play a joke on a new headmaster by turning the bell upside down and filling it with water, so that when he rang it, he was soaked. Nathaniel Jones, a schoolmaster in the early 1800s, remarks in his memoirs that the students at Warwick were "undisciplined!"

The first documentation of a school carrying the name "Warwick" is The Warwick Seminary, conducted by Edward V. Coulton by 1840. In 1854, the Warwick Institute was built as the Warwick Academy, a private school. It stood on High Street toward Forester Avenue, where currently there is a parking lot for Warwick Valley Telecommunications. It became Warwick Institute, and was turned over to the Board of Education in 1860, but not without a fight on the part of taxpayers who did not want to fund it. In 1906, the high school classes had 56 students. Teachers and some students boarded at the Wawayanda Hotel. The school was first built of wood, but later was rebuilt of brick. The old wooden building was moved toward the creek, and renamed "The White Elephant" building.[51] It was used as apartments until it became derelict and was torn down.

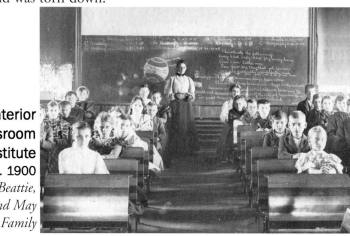

**Interior Classroom Warwick Institute
c. 1900**
Collection of Beattie, Jacob, and May Family

The Historical Society of the Town of Warwick

Warwick Institute Students
1906
Photographed by F. J. Welles
Historical Society of the Town of Warwick

Entire student body of the Warwick Institute gathered on the banks of the Wawayanda Creek, after the institute had been rebuilt of brick.

The Warwick Institute
After 1893
Historical Society of the Town of Warwick

The brick building, which replaced the wooden structure, was built in 1893. Once Warwick's first high school was built on Welling Avenue, this school building was used as a grammar school until it burned down on February 1, 1951.

193

The Warwick Institute Upper Class Members and Staff
After 1893
Historical Society of the Town of Warwick

Hylah Hasbrouck is the probable identity of the girl on the far right of seated row.

Warwick High School
c. 1910
Historical Society of the Town of Warwick

Warwick's first High School stood on Welling Avenue on the left-hand side of the current Doc Fry Community Center. It is no longer standing.[52]

Warwick Valley Junior & Senior High
c. 1930
Historical Society of the Town of Warwick

The new Warwick Valley Junior and Senior High School was built on Park Avenue, on the edge of a new development called "Hathorn Park," and is now known as Park Avenue Elementary School. Voters approved its building in September of 1928. The arguments for the need of a new school were so strong that the papers reported no objections to it before the favorable vote was taken.

The Manor House
New York City Farm
c. 1914-1918
Historical Society of the Town of Warwick

One of the nation's first substance abuse programs was run by the City of New York at the old Wisner/Durland farm on Wickham Lake. The land was purchased by Capt. John Wisner in 1766 as part of the Perry's Pond tract, an old name for Wickham Lake. His brother was Henry Wisner, who attended the Continental Congress and missed signing the *Declaration of Independence* because he rushed home to Middletown to begin manufacturing much-needed gunpowder. This manor house was built on the foundations of a pre-Revolutionary War home around 1850 by Henry Board Wisner. The City spent at least $1 million on the facility. The Farm's innovative approach treated alcohol and drug addiction as a clinical disease, an idea which was new at the time. Inmates were prescribed a regimen of clean living, outdoor exercise, and work. [53]

Camp Colony and Brick House
New York City Farm
1914-1918
Collection of the Simms Family

We do not know whether the camp colony was used as overflow housing in warm weather, or if part of the regular regimen at the camp included outdoor sleeping in summer.

State Training School
c. 1930s
Historical Society of the Town of Warwick

After the closure of the New York City Farm, the State of New York bought the property and ran another groundbreaking social program: The New York State Training School for Boys. This reform school served as an alternative to jail time for youthful offenders. Begun in 1932, it continued until 1976, when it was closed and tranformed into the Mid State Correctional Facility.[54]

Shrine at State Training School
c. 1930s
Historical Society of the Town of Warwick

The Boys' School was a high-profile program, and when the shrine that the boys built was dedicated, Eleanor Roosevelt came to participate and have tea.

The First Lady Visits the Boys' School

My Day, June 28, 1945

Reprinted from the Eleanor Roosevelt Estate Papers with Permission of Nancy Roosevelt Ireland

HYDE PARK, Wednesday—Now that I am home permanently, one of the first things I wanted to do was to see again the State Training School for Boys at Warwick, New York, the institution in which I was much interested years ago during my husband's time in Albany. Yesterday I was able to do this with Mrs. Sidney Sherwood, who is a member of the Board of Visitors, and to observe the conditions that now prevail.

On the physical side, the plant has greatly improved. I remember the cottages as bare brick buildings; today the planting around them is lovely. There were practically no shops for vocational training or for work then. Today the most finished equipment is installed. Boys who work in these shops could learn a trade for use in their future lives.

In talking to the dietician, however, I found that the children are fed on 40 cents a day. The boys I saw yesterday, I should judge, ranged in age from 12 to 16, with most of them apparently between 14 and 16. Some of them looked much older than their years; others are not so well developed physically. But few of the faces are youthful.

They run a farm, and so they grow some of their vegetables, and they have a glass of milk at breakfast and at supper. But I gathered that the cost of production is counted in on that 40 cents. Even if you had a family of between four and five hundred, and could buy wholesale, you would find that you could not do very well at 40 cents per day per head.

Sometimes I wish that the housewives of the state had a representative serving on budget committees which decide on what is to be spent in state institutions. I was firmly told by Dr. Williams that this allowance was in line with the allowances of other state institutions. Yet any mother of boys knows that they need more food than the average grown person.

I was therefore not surprised to find, when I had a chance to talk to the boys, that they responded more quickly when I asked them what they liked to eat. They have meat on Sundays and fish on Fridays. Eggs or cheese or beans are the rule on the other days, I gather, with chopped meat occasionally thrown in. Even on Christmas last year they did not have ice cream, and most of us who have youngsters around a great deal know what a favorite dessert this is. You can do a lot with children through food, but it must be rather hard to do it on 40 cents per head. The staff gets an allowance of 80 cents, but some of this money is spent for service.

Those of you who have not been interested in your training schools for boys and girls in your state may want to go and visit them. After all, these boys are either going to be good citizens in the future, or else you are going to pay for them in penal institutions permanently. Tomorrow I'll tell you more about Warwick.

Eleanor Roosevelt

State Training School for Boys
c. 1930s
Collection of Betty Zacharewicz

The boys were organized into "cottages," with each building having a house mother and father who supervised the group. The program was considered a model for similar facilities. Before cottages were completed in 1933, the boys slept in a wooden bunkhouse. Students were often from the most impoverished and violent backgrounds in the New York metro area. They were given a few months in a highly structured, much more safe environment to see if they could adapt to a new life.

The experiences of two of the former inmates made it into print: Claude Brown's autobiographical *Manchild in the Promised Land*, and a biography of Conrad E. Mauge, Jr. by Ira Freeman, *Out of the Burning*. Both are considered classics of African American literature.

My Day, June 29, 1945

Reprinted from the Eleanor Roosevelt Estate Papers with Permission of Nancy Roosevelt Ireland

HYDE PARK, Thursday — As I said yesterday, the shops at the Warwick State Training School for Boys are very beautifully equipped, and the boys who work in them were enthusiastic about the possibilities of learning a trade. But one of our party, who looked in at the carpenter shop, said it appeared as though it was not often used. On inquiry, we found that at present there was difficulty in getting materials for the boys to work with.

We were shown a room in which commercial art was being taught, and were told that about eight boys usually made up the class. Only such boys as showed talent enough to make it probable that they would earn a living at this type of work were allowed to spend here the five hours a day allotted to the project. When we asked whether artistic expression sometimes did not have therapeutic value for boys without special talent, we were told that undoubtedly it had, and even much disturbed children improved when they had the release of artistic expression. Nevertheless, the usual class was eight and it was limited to boys showing real talent.

I inquired whether band music or group singing were a part of the training in the arts, since music and dancing would probably be two of the most popular forms of artistic expression where the percentage of colored boys is so high. I could not find that either one was a part of the training or the recreational program.

We learned that one bath a week is the rule in the cottages — at least, it is the rule in the one our party visited. I imagine their theory coincides with my grandmother's. When we were children, a Saturday night hot bath was all that was required of us, although we did have to sponge off with cold water every morning. We were fairly active children; but we were not doing eight hours of work, which many of these boys are doing both on the grounds and for farmers in the neighborhood. The boys like the work and, when it is not too heavy, I am sure it is good for them. But I don't see why, in these days, there has to be a rule curtailing baths unless the water supply is low.

Dr. Williams has always seemed to me a charming person, with impeccable theories. Yet I came away with the feeling that someone in authority was showing very little real love and understanding toward the boys. Of course, there are bad boys. But what has made them so? I should like to pursue this further tomorrow.

Eleanor Roosevelt

First Hay Rake
State Training School for Boys
c. 1930
Collection of Betty Zacharewicz

Part of the regimen prescribed for the boys involved manual labor in the fresh air. This shows the first hay rake purchased for the farm. Haying was part of the agricultural program at the school.

Haywagon
State Training School for Boys
c. 1930s
Collection of Betty Zacharewicz

Gathering Hay
State Training School for Boys
c. 1930s
Collection of Betty Zacharewicz

Some boys were brought to the school as early as June 1930 to begin working on the facility and the development of the programs. Most of them had never had even a glimpse of a rural landscape, and cows and horses were a completely new experience.

First Hay Stack
State Training School for Boys
c. 1932
Collection of Betty Zacharewicz

Sherwood Hall
c. 1925
Historical Society of the Town of Warwick

Sherwood Hall, now known as the Warwick Conference Center off Hoyt Road, started in 1921. The New York Telephone Company operated a combination sanitorium and fresh air camp for their operators on the grounds of the old Hoyt homestead. As early as 1908 it had been recognized that the women were at increased risk for tuberculosis and other communicable diseases, for they worked in large hot rooms packed with operators, and shared headsets. In 1944, it was purchased from NY Telephone by R. H. Macy Company, and operated as their employee camp for many years.

Camp Sherwood
c. 1925
Historical Society of the Town of Warwick

Above: hiking at Camp Sherwood. Below: basket weaving.

Sherwood Hall Dairy Barns
c. 1925
Historical Society of the Town of Warwick, Joslyn Collection

The dairy barns at Sherwood Hall provided fresh milk and butter.

Warwick Hospital
c. 1920
Historical Society of the Town of Warwick

The Warwick Hospital on Forester Avenue in Warwick was established by Dr. H. K. Bradner and his son Dr. Morris Renfrew Bradner by leasing the property known as the Servin Mansion from Mrs. Albert Burk in November of 1915. The hospital opened in May of 1916.

The Arches
c. 1915
Historical Society of the Town of Warwick

The Arches, home of Grinnell Burt at Grand Street and Oakland Avenue in Warwick, became part of St. Anthony Community Hospital. Purchased by the Sisters of the Poor in 1937 with the intention of forming a hospital, it soon became clear that it was inadequate and plans for an additional facility were made.

St. Anthony Community Hospital
c. 1940
Historical Society of the Town of Warwick

St. Anthony Community Hospital was built in cooperation with Dr. Morris Renfrew Bradner. The Warwick General Hospital had by that time become inadequate and in danger of losing its payments from insurance carriers due to its inability to expand and update. Talks between Mother Aquilina and Dr. Bradner produced an accord, and funding was secured. The new hospital was dedicated in April of 1939, with over 2,500 people attending the ceremony.[55]

Hospitality & Tourism

Baird's Tavern
c. 1900
Historical Society of the Town of Warwick

Baird's Tavern, located on Main Street in Warwick, was built in 1766 by Francis Baird, who saw opportunity in a way station here on the King's Highway, one of the major routes between Philadelphia and Boston. It paid off, and many colonial era travelers stopped here, including George Washington, in July of 1782. In this photo it was owned by William Benjamin Sayer.[56]

Wawayanda House
c. 1860s
Historical Society of the Town of Warwick

Wawayanda House stood at the corner of Forester and Colonial Avenues. In the mid 1800s Henry William Herbert ("Frank Forester"), author of *Warwick Woodlands,* visited often. The inn was run by his friend Thomas Ward.[57]

Wawayanda House
c. 1890-1905
Historical Society of the Town of Warwick, Joslyn Collection

Later in its history, the hotel became the boarding house for the Warwick Institute, and was eventually torn down. The lower level was below ground until the road was cut down to put in a water system. A section of the railings are included in the duplex home which now stands on this site.

The Historical Society of the Town of Warwick

Warwick Valley House
c. 1880
Collection of Bill Raynor

The Warwick Valley House on Oakland Avenue was built in 1862 by M. F. Ten Eyck to serve travelers brought by the new Warwick Valley Railroad. Today it is known as the Dispatch Building. This shot also shows the Joseph Smith livery stable to the right. The Warwick Valley House changed hands several times: by 1907 the proprietor was Ed Ryerson, and the livery stable in back was run by Van Ness; then later by Joseph Smith.[58]

Germania House Hotel and Rightmeyer's Drug Store
c. 1915
Historical Society of the Town of Warwick

What is now Akin's at the corner of McEwen and Main in Warwick has always been a pharmacy, starting with the Rightmeyers in 1899. Also, the upper floors were once the Germania House hotel owned by Mr. and Mrs. Albert Burk.[59]

Days Gone By   A History in Pictures Town of Warwick, New York 1827-1945

National Hotel and Demerest Hall
1875
Historical Society of the Town of Warwick

With the railroad came a surge in visitors and travelers. Located just across from the Railroad Station, it was built October 1865 by Thomas Demerest. Later a large recreation hall was added. Famous for its applejack, served at a huge wooden bar, balls and dances as well as lectures were held here, and it became the social and cultural center of the village. The wooden hotel burned in 1887, shortly after it was sold. Thomas Demerest repurchased the property and built a larger, more elegant brick hotel with gas lights. The elegant bar room rivaled the finest in New York City. The brick building still stands and has recently had its facade renovated in keeping with its historic past.[60]

Elaborate Bar at Demerest Hall
After 1887
Historical Society of the Town of Warwick

Demerest Building
1907-1914
Historical Society of the Town of Warwick

Railroad Avenue, Warwick
c. 1900
Historical Society of the Town of Warwick, Joslyn Collection

Location, location, location! Railroad Avenue rolls out the welcome mat for visitors and travelers. Newly rebuilt Demerest House on left, Demerest Hall for meetings and "conventions," and a store to pick-up basic essentials to and from your destination.[61]

Welling House
c. 1890
Florida Historical Society

Welling House stood at the southwest corner of Welling Place and Main Street, at what is now the location of the Warwick Valley Telephone Company. This photo is looking west, down Welling Place. The sign reads, "Wm. A. Randall, Proprietor."

The Red Swan Inn
c. 1910
Historical Society of the Town of Warwick

The Red Swan Inn was constructed in 1902. Designed by Clinton Wheeler Wisner, with architect Ernest G.W. Dietrich, it was the one of the largest and most luxurious accommodations built during the high point of Warwick's early tourism industry.

Rear View of The Red Swan Inn
c. 1910
Collection of James Cline

Red Swan Inn Staff
c. 1910-1915
Historical Society of the Town of Warwick, Joslyn Collection

Is one of your grandparents in this group? Many locals worked at the inn at one time or another.

Red Swan Tourist Coach
c. 1910
Historical Society of the Town of Warwick, Joslyn Collection

The tourist coach, at Galloway Road intersection was run by the Wisner brothers for the Red Swan. A story is told that as an added thrill, one trip included a fake "hold up"—however, it was too much excitement for the passengers, and was not tried again!

A Cozy Nook at the Red Swan Inn
c. 1915
Historical Society of the Town of Warwick

The motto on the fireplace is an excerpt from *The Great Lone Land: A Narrative of Travel and Adventure in the North-West of America* by W. F. Butler, 1872 where he is describing a Native American canoe:

"And the forest life is in it, All its mystery and its magic, All the tightness of the birch-tree, All the toughness of the cedar, All the larch's supple sinews. And it floated on the river like a yellow leaf in autumn, Like a yellow water-lily."

The designers of the Red Swan Inn used references to Native Americans several times, to express their reverence for the First People and the historic site of Mistucky, sleeping under the fields across the street.

Schoolcraft's Legend OF THE RED SWAN

"THREE brothers were hunting on a wager to see who would bring home the first game. "They were to shoot no other animal," the legend says, "but such as each was in the habit of killing. They set out different ways: Odjibwa, the youngest, had not gone far before he saw a bear, an animal he was not to kill, by the agreement. He followed him close, and drove an arrow through him which brought him to the ground.

"ALTHOUGH contrary to the bet, he immediately commenced skinning him, when suddenly something red tinged all the air around him. He rubbed his eyes, thinking he was perhaps deceived; but without effect for the red hue continued. At length he heard a strange noise at a distance. It first appeared like a human voice, but after following the sound for some distance, he reached the shores of a lake, and soon saw the object he was looking for.

"AT a distance out in the lake sat a most beautiful Red Swan, whose plumage glittered in the sun, and who would now and then make the same noise he had heard. He was within long bow-shot, and, pulling the arrow from the bowstring up to his ear, took deliberate aim and shot. The arrow took no effect; and he shot and shot again till his quiver was empty. Still the swan remained, moving round and round, stretching its long neck and dipping its bill into the water, as if heedless of the arrows shot at it.

"ODJIBWA ran home, and got all his own and his brother's arrows, and shot them all away. He then stood and gazed at the beautiful bird. While standing, he remembered his brother's saying that in their deceased father's medicine-sack were three magic arrows. Off he started, his anxiety to kill the swan overcoming all scruples. At any other time, he would have deemed it sacrilege to open his father's medicine-sack; but now he hastily seized the three arrows and ran back, leaving the other contents of the sack scattered over the lodge. The swan was still there.

"HE shot the first arrow with great precision, and came very near to it. The second came still closer; as he took the last arrow, he felt his arm firmer, and, drawing it up with vigor, saw it pass through the neck of the swan a little above the breast. Still it did not prevent the bird from flying off, which it did, however, at first slowly, flapping its wings and rising gradually into the air, and then flying off toward the sinking of the sun."

"Into this old tradition," writes Longfellow "I have woven other curious Indian legends, drawn chiefly from the various and valuable writings of Mr Schoolcraft, to whom the literary world is greatly indebted."

"Can it be the sun descending
O'er the level plain of water?
Or the Red Swan floating, flying,
Wounded by the magic arrow."
— SONG OF HIAWATHA

Legend of the Red Swan
c. 1905-1915
Historical Society of the Town of Warwick, Joslyn Collection

This photo is of probably either a sign at the Red Swan Inn, or of a poster that was printed for their use. The legend is usually concluded: "From that time forth, just at sunset, the blood of the wounded swan cast a blush, like the rich color of a maiden's cheek, over the surface of the waters."

Aspell House in Florida
c. 1900
Florida Historical Society

Florida taverns were popular in the 18th century when John Kennedy kept a tavern in this building, at 32 North Main Street in Florida, one of the oldest hotels in Orange County. Known as the Aspell House as early as 1859, it prospered through the early days of the 20th century, but fell into decline during the prohibition years.

The Dill House in Florida
c. 1905
Reprinted from Florida Historical book [2]

The Dill House was another of Florida's busy tourist facilities. Five chimneys served the hearths which provided warmth for the guest rooms, the restaurant, and the ballroom.

The Dill House Era
c. 1905
Reprinted from Florida Historical book [2]

In the 1920s and early 1930s you could still relax in the shade of the huge elm in front of the Dill House and listen to the Florida Firemen's Band, directed by Floyd Quackenbush, playing favorite selections in the gazebo on the Presbyterian Church lawn. That, figuratively speaking, was the "swan song" of the Dill House era.

Pine Island Hotel
1918
Collection of Barbara Morgiewicz

The Pine Island Hotel was established in the hamlet by 1859, run by William Wilcox.

Ferncliff Hotel, Greenwood Lake
c. 1915
Collection of Nina Steen

Located on the west shore, the Ferncliff Hotel was the largest hotel at the lake. Originally built as a private hotel by the Greenwood Lake Association around 1877, it became the Ferncliff around 1891. Fire destroyed the hotel in the 1920s; only the boathouse survived, which is now a private residence.[62]

Brandon House, Greenwood Lake
c. 1915
Collection of Nina Steen

The Brandon House, located on the east shore of Greenwood Lake, was built by Alexander Brandon in 1870. It was a typical grand hotel. Not all those who came were concerned with the social amenities and boating, however. One visitor was Louis S. Kohler, who studied birds at the lake over a long time period in the 1910s. He wrote up his list of species in the *Wilson Bulletin*, September 1922. It included such rarities as the Bohemian Waxwing, which does not normally come into southern New York.

Organizations

YMCA in Warwick
c. 1915
Historical Society of the Town of Warwick

The Warwick Young Men's Christian Association (YMCA) was founded in 1879. For many years the 1810 House on Main Street was the home of the local branch of the YMCA, and hosted many social improvement programs such as a gymnasium and a library. The Women's Auxiliary was founded in May of 1886. One of their services was helping find care for the sick, prior to establishment of the hospital. The Barker House on Church Street was one place used as a convalescence home for patients with tuberculosis.

Warwick Cemetery
c. 1870s
Historical Society of the Town of Warwick

The Warwick Cemetery Association provided the community a common site for burial and remembrance of the departed. Prior to its formation, burials were in many separate association and family plots. This shows the original gates, which are now long gone. This image is from a stereograph.

Albert Wisner Memorial Library
c. 1930
Historical Society of the Town of Warwick

Albert Wisner Memorial Library was built in 1927, as a bequest from Mrs. Albert Wisner in memory of her husband, a Warwick native who went west and made a fortune helping to rebuild Chicago after the great fire. This image shows the Frank Forester monument and the Sanford Fountain.

Masonic Lodge No. 544
c. 1920 (left) and 1928 (right)
Collection of Bill Raynor

Masonic Lodge No. 544 building is on the corner of West and Main. The Warwick lodge was chartered in 1864. They rented the third floor of the building on the left in 1878, and purchased the building in 1923. The building was remodeled in 1928 (top right photo). The old traffic light in the road was known as the "dead man," because it was hit so many times.

Haymakers' Gathering
c. 1900
Collection of Bill Raynor

A Haymakers' gathering in front of the Demerest House. The group was an adjunct of the Improved Order of the Red Men, which had a lodge here in Warwick. The local branch was the Tuxedo Tribe of the Red Men, organized around 1895. They had a membership of over 100 in 1907. Among their projects was payment of sick and burial benefits for their members. Theodore H. June, a local man, was State president in 1904.[63]

Warwick Cornet Band
c. 1915
Historical Society of the Town of Warwick, Joslyn Collection

The Warwick Cornet Band poses in front of Village Hall. Formed in 1878, most of the same fifteen founders were still members in 1881. Another photo was run by the *Warwick Dispatch* in January of 1940.

Warwick Glider Club
c. 1930s
Historical Society of the Town of Warwick

The Warwick Glider Club was formed in the 1930s by a group of friends who acquired a wooden glider. They would launch from Mt. Peter using rubber shock cords, and frequently land down below in Houston's field. The late John W. Sanford, Jr. was a founding member, and his first pilot's license was signed by Orville Wright. Other members included John Lucha, Richard "Dick" Seely, Thomas and Virginia Lawrence, mechanic Earl Stidworthy and flight instructor and airport administrator William "Willie" Falck. In 1936, with the aid of a federal grant, the Warwick Municipal Airport opened.[64]

A plane landing at Warwick was a sight many rushed to see. The auto is possibly a Packard.

Plane Landing at Warwick
c. 1930
Historical Society of the Town of Warwick, Joslyn Collection

The Historical Society of the Town of Warwick

Excelsior Hose No. 1
c. 1875
Historical Society of the Town of Warwick

Excelsior Hose No. 1 was founded in 1869 and incorporated in 1888. Here they gather near their firehouse on High Street, at the corner of High and Main, in front of what is now Lewis Park. The house was taken down in 1956 or 1957 as part of the creation of Lewis Park.[65]

Raymond Hose No. 2
c. 1900
Historical Society of the Town of Warwick

Raymond Hose was founded in 1896. Their first home was a building on the grounds of the Fabric Fire Hose Company, donated for their use by the company president, Mr. Raymond.

Goodwill Hook & Ladder
c. 1900
Historical Society of the Town of Warwick

Goodwill Hook and Ladder was founded in 1890; their fire house was in the Village Hall (old Dutch Reformed Church) until the Forester Avenue fire house was completed.

Fire Departments

The first fire department organized in town was Excelsior in 1869; then Florida in 1886; Goodwill Hook and Ladder in 1890; and then Raymond Hose in 1896. The Pioneer Fire Co. in Greenwood Lake was operating by 1907, Pine Island in 1935, Amity in 1947, and Engine Co. No. 3 in 1967.

Excelsior Fire House
c. 1900
Historical Society of the Town of Warwick

Home of the Excelsiors, Warwick's first fire department was on High Street, now owned by Judge Peter Barlet and used for his private law practice. The old siren is clearly visible on the roof.

Raymond Hose Fire House
c. 1900
Historical Society of the Town of Warwick

Finished in the spring of 1901, the structure on Howe Street was used as the Raymond Hose company's home until 2005, when the new building on West Street was completed.

Florida's Highland Engine and Hose Co. No. 3
c. 1900
Photograph by James Razey
Reprinted from Florida Historical book [2]

On December 5, 1885, sixteen residents of Florida met to form a volunteer fire company. The first fire equipment consisted of a dozen pails, painted red, some ice pike poles used to pull or push over burning walls, a few axes, crowbars, and some lanterns.

In 1887, the company purchased a twenty-man power fire pump (drawn by a team of horses or by hand) from the Highland Engine and Hose Co. No. 3 of the City of Newburgh, on the condition that Florida had to take the name of Highland Engine and Hose Co. No. 3. In the photograph above, fireman Samuel Green is seated second from the left. J. K. Roe is standing second from the right.

Sandford Fire Trucks
c. 1930
Reprinted from Florida Historical book [2]

This postcard shows two Sanford fire trucks, a 1928 and 1929, side by side, in front of the fire house at 19 South Main Street in Florida. Due to the dedication of Bill Jayne, the 1929 Sanford was returned to Florida and recently restored.

The Sunshine Society
c. 1909
Reprinted from Florida Historical book [2]

The Sunshine Society poses in front of the Fire House/Telephone Company.

Railroads

Grinnell Burt
c. 1880
Engraving from Cyclopedia of National Biography

Grinnell Burt (1822-1901) was one of the founders of the Warwick Valley Railroad Company in 1859 and served as its President for the first 41 years. Born and raised in Warwick, he and others founded the railroad to link the local agricultural and dairy industry with broader markets in the region, and to encourage growth and prosperity for the Town. The home he built, "The Arches," still stands as part of the St. Anthony Community Hospital complex.[67]

Engine No. 1
The Grinnell Burt
c. 1890-1900
Historical Society of the Town of Warwick, Published in Warwick Historical Papers

Engine No. 1 was dubbed "The 'Grinnell Burt" by the Lehigh and Hudson River Railway (L&HRR). The Warwick Valley Railroad never owned any locomotives; instead, they used Erie equipment. This picture of Engine No. 1 was taken after it had been converted from a wood burner to coal-fired.

Warwick Train Station
1887-1893
Historical Society of the Town of Warwick

Warwick's first railroad station on Railroad Avenue became the new hub of activity for the village—the previous hub had been clustered at the north end near the intersection of Colonial Avenue and Main. Lower Main Street had wet areas that bred mosquitoes. Note the low-tech pest control on top of the building—a purple martin house.

The Historical Society of the Town of Warwick

Train By Warwick Institute
March 12, 1891
Photographed by John M. Servin
Collection of Marty Feldner

Looking from Forester Avenue we see a coal hauler with wooden cars and a small center cab locomotive. Large building in background appears to be the Warwick Institute.

Warwick Coal Tower
c. 1910-1915
Historical Society of the Town of Warwick, Joslyn Collection

Coal was brought in on the elevated center track, dumped into a trough under the track, and then lifted to the top of the bunkers by an elevator in the "towers" on either side of the structure. The chute was lowered by a rope and a gate was opened to send a load of coal to the tender.

New Milford Depot
c. 1910
Collection of Casper and Terry Hann

At stops along the new railroad, depot buildings and other commercial enterprises sprang up. At New Milford, local businesses prospered with the increased customer traffic. Typically a depot would have an office where the stationmaster worked, passengers could buy amenities, and an area or separate building where freight could be stored.

New Milford Depot
c. 1910
Collection of Casper and Terry Hann

Back view of depot and freight storage building.

Railroad Avenue in Warwick
c. 1915-1920
Historical Society of the Town of Warwick, Joslyn Collection

Railroad Avenue in Warwick grew as the railroad grew, and brought visitors, business travelers, and freight in and out of town. In addition to the Demerest House and the Warwick Valley House, the Railroad Hotel (later known as Billy Barnes' Turf Exchange) also operated in close proximity to the station. Here we also see the Warwick Auto Company, and the Hynard Brothers' store.

South Street Railroad Yard
c. 1905-1918
Collection of Marty Feldner

An everyday scene at the busy depot. On left is milk boxcar number 28 which went into service sometime after 1905. Above the buggy is the old railroad station, which was moved and reused as the railyard office.

Loading the Coal Tender at Warwick
1915
Historical Society of the Town of Warwick, Joslyn Collection

The "camelback" or center cab type of engine was found only on northeastern anthracite coal railroads. The unique design was made necessary by the hard anthracite coal, which required a very wide firebox at the rear of the boiler, leaving no room for a cab in the usual rear position.

Railway Gun
c. 1915
Historical Society of the Town of Warwick, Joslyn Collection

A crowd collects as a railway gun pauses at the Elm Street yard, next to the machine shop. Rails presented the perfect transport and firing platform for land-based large ordnance. The gun could be moved relatively quickly along the rail system and the recoil could be dispersed by allowing the carriage to move back down the tracks (sometimes up to 100 feet). They were first used in the Civil War. These guns could fire up to thirty miles and were capable of reaching far into the enemy's rear positions. This gun, likely built by Baldwin Locomotive Works in Philadelphia during WWI, appears to be on its way to New England for embarkation. The building in the background is probably the sawmill of Martin Van Buren Horton, for whom Van Buren Street was named.

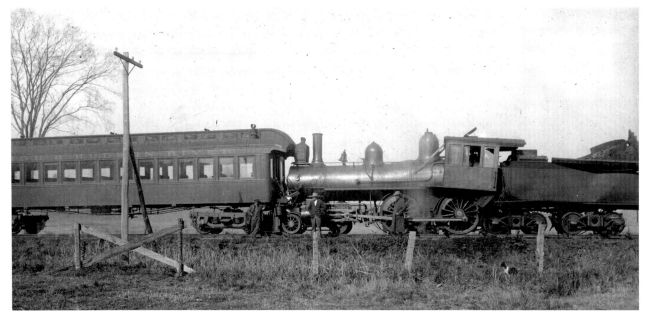

Train Wreck
c. 1915
Historical Society of the Town of Warwick, Joslyn Collection

The railroad was not without its mishaps. Here an engine and a passenger car have collided.

New Milford Station Complex
c. 1910
Historical Society of the Town of Warwick

Conklin and Strong was one of the "anchor" businesses in the New Milford station complex as well as at several other stations.

New Warwick Railroad Station
c. 1910-1920
Historical Society of the Town of Warwick

Warwick's train station was built in 1893.

Train Arrives at Warwick Station
c. 1910-1920
Historical Society of the Town of Warwick

"Just in" at Warwick's Railroad Station—the arrival of a train is something that the whole village would have been aware of.

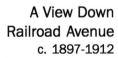

A View Down Railroad Avenue
c. 1897-1912
Historical Society of the Town of Warwick, Joslyn Collection

This view down Railroad Avenue shows the station and a stack in the center background, which appears to be that of the Warwick Valley Light and Power Company generating station.

Lake Station Depot
c. 1900
Collection of the Simms Family

The Lake Station work crew takes a break after unloading, and passengers wait to embark. This appears to be the original station. About 1910-1911, all stations between Warwick and Greycourt were replaced with larger buildings, all identical. The depot in Sugar Loaf, by the caboose, is one of the replacement stations.

New Railroad Office Under Construction
c. 1909
Historical Society of the Town of Warwick, Joslyn Collection

In July of 1907, the railroad purchased an additional 25 acres of land on River Street in Warwick for a new yard, roundhouse, and offices. The land had at one time housed a race track run by G. W. Hyatt. This building currently houses private offices.

Completed New Railroad Office
c. 1910
Historical Society of the Town of Warwick

New Roundhouse
c. 1913-1915
Historical Society of the Town of Warwick, Joslyn Collection

New roundhouse, with gondola car, at Elm Street. The dark building on left became Kinney's Market.

Railroad Yard Complex
c. 1940-1950
Collection of Marty Feldner

Railroad yard complex on River Street included the coal tower, roundhouse, and storehouse (right). At this point, the railroad is still primarily a steam operation, but diesel engines are beginning to be used.

Flood of 1903
c. 1903
Historical Society of the Town of Warwick

During the early 1900s, the railroad was a vital link not only for our citizens and the local dairy farmers, but also regionally for moving coal supplies from Pennsylvania to the industrial centers of New England. The devastating flood of 1903 washed out tracks and bridges in a wide area. This image shows the South Street railroad yard. Passenger service ended in the summer of 1939.[68]

Flood of 1903
c. 1903
Historical Society of the Town of Warwick

A tactic used to help save bridges from washing away was to park an engine on the bridge itself. The added weight often preserved the structure.

L&HRR Crane No. 100
c. 1915
Historical Society of the Town of Warwick

Another type of mishap the railroad sometimes fell prey to was a train wreck. This "wrecking" crane was in use up until the 1960s.

The Historical Society of the Town of Warwick

Warwick Railroad Office
Before 1901
Historical Society of the Town of Warwick

The railroad wouldn't have existed without the people that made it run. Here Grinnell Burt sits in the old railroad office on Main Street, in the building that later became Town Hall and now houses the Toy Chest store, near the corner of South Street.

Grinnell Burt Funeral
c. 1901
Collection of Christ Church

An elaborate procession stretched down Main Street.

L&HRR Officer Meeting
c. 1920s
Collection of Marty Feldner

Officers of the L&HRR meet at the old Mt. Peter House.

L&HRR Shop Workers
c. 1920-1925
Collection of Marty Feldner

Without the workers, the railroad would not have run. Here workers at the rail yard at the Warwick shops take a break for a rare portrait.

Lake Station
c. 1910
Collection of the Simms Family

At Lake Station, workers take a break before heading off on the handcar.

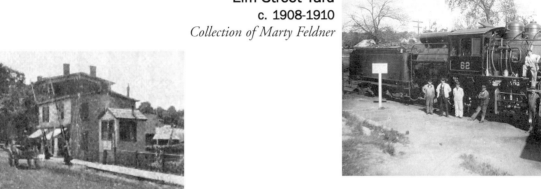

Crew with Engine 62
Elm Street Yard
c. 1908-1910
Collection of Marty Feldner

Oakland Crossing
c. 1910
Historical Society of the Town of Warwick

Before electrical signals, a flag was waved or a manual gate was lowered at crossings to stop the flow of traffic. The life of a crossing signalman wasn't an easy one; lives depended on his continual alertness. The signalman's shack, which was manned by Barney Diffily, is at the right side in this image of the Oakland Avenue crossing in Warwick.

Barney Diffily, Signalman
c. 1880s
Courtesy of Michael Diffily

For each of the hundreds of employees of the railroad, there is a story. One of the keepers of the Warwick Main Street crossing was Barney Diffily, who emigrated from Ireland around 1860. In the 1880s and 1890s Railroad Green was known fondly as "Diffily's Park," for he tended the area and kept a large garden there. He eventually moved to Asheville, NY, near the home of the Chautauqua movement, and became an avid attender of its Literary and Science course.[69]

Days Gone By   A History in Pictures Town of Warwick, New York 1827-1945

Florida Station Complex
c. 1905
Reprinted from Florida Historical book [2]

Florida was a station of the Erie's Pine Island Branch when this picture was taken, around the turn of the century. This branch was built in 1868 and was in running condition during 1869. It ran from Goshen to the southern portion of Orange County, and did a heavy business in carrying milk, butter, and cheese. Railroad Hotel, in the center foreground, was doing a thriving business as was the Borden's Condensery, pictured behind the hotel. This complex was loacated at the intersection of Maple Avenue and Jayne Street.

Pine Island Train Station
c. 1915
Collection of Barbara Morgiewicz

Florida Depot
c. 1910
Historical Society of the Town of Warwick

The Erie station in Florida was located at the end of Jayne Street.

The Historical Society of the Town of Warwick

Sterling Forest Depot & Landing, Greenwood Lake
c. 1915
Collection of Nina Steen

The Sterling Forest Depot and Landing in Greenwood Lake was just over the border into New Jersey. It was served by a branch of the Erie Railroad called the Greenwood Lake and Montclair Railroad. It was built in 1875, and the tracks took the path of what is now East Shore Road. In its day it contributed greatly to the growth of Greenwood Lake as a tourist destination. The last train ran on September 28, 1935.[70]

Waiting
c. 1915
Historical Society of the Town of Warwick, Joslyn Collection

A switchman waits in the gloom of dawn or dusk.

Sports

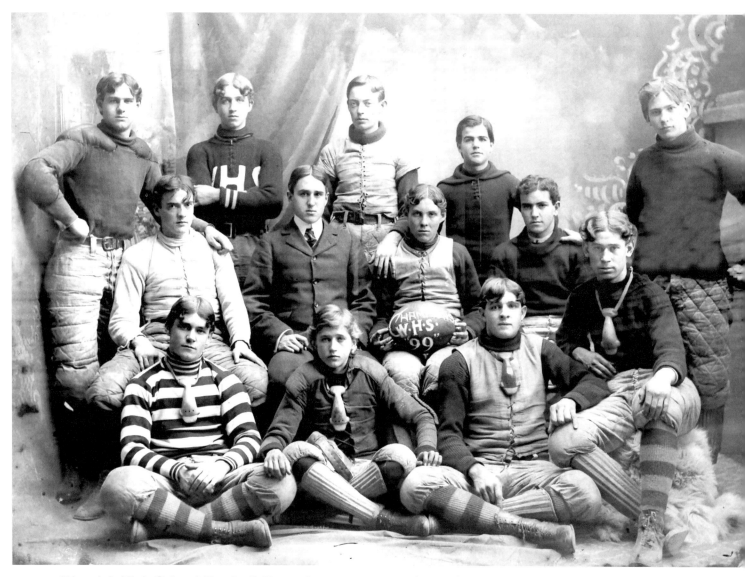

Warwick High School Football Champions
1899
Historical Society of the Town of Warwick, Joslyn Collection

Pride in the accomplishments of local sports teams is not a recent phenomenon! Athletics has played a large part of our educational system and youth development for many generations. Although clothing styles have changed, the intensity and promise shining out of teenage faces is something that will always be the same.

One of the advantages of the large format of the glass plate negatives (this one is 8"x10") is that a great deal of detail is preserved. It is fun to think about how each of these young men would have responded to a mundane question like, "So, what are your plans for the future?" They are each, so clearly and forever, individuals.

We do not know who is who, but these last names are listed as playing on the team that year: Weeden, Miller, Still, Morris, Benedict, Clark, Lawrence, Baily, Luchi, Decker, and John Longwell, who went on to play for Ohio University's team.

The first documented football team in the Warwick schools was a few years prior, in 1896.

The Historical Society of the Town of Warwick

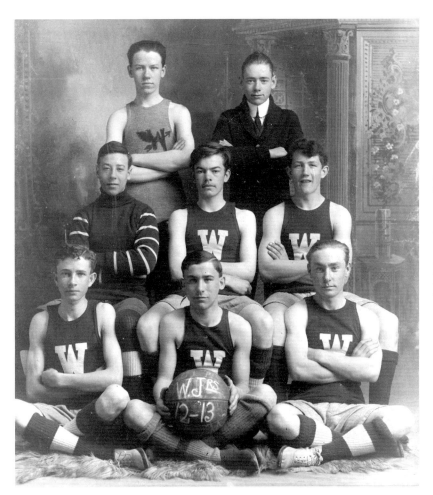

**Junior Varsity Basketball Team
Warwick High School
1913**
Historical Society of the Town of Warwick, Joslyn Collection

Note early team logo on shirt, enlarged above.

**Girls' Basketball Team
Warwick High School
1904**
Historical Society of the Town of Warwick, Joslyn Collection

237

1901-1903 Track Team
S. S. Seward Institute
c. 1903
Collection of John and Dorothy Kimiecik

Florida S. S. Seward Institute Track Team 1901, 1902, 1903. Shown is Principal G. C. Schaible and the team: E. A. Quackenbush, Irving Weed, and Roy G. Wisner.

1930-31 Basketball Team
S. S. Seward Institute
c. 1931
Collection of John and Dorothy Kimiecik

1930-1931 S. S. Seward Institute (Florida) Basketball Team consisted of:

Front Row: Harold Sakofsky, Lou Borkowski, Charles Plock, Charles Stoll, Don DeKay

Back Row: John Wisniewski (Manager), Adam Regelski, Chick Ehlers, James Boyd, Ignatius Garvilla, Leonard Nash (Coach/Principal)

1946-47 Basketball Team
S. S. Seward Institute
c. 1947
Collection of John and Dorothy Kimiecik

Front Row: Clarence Myruski, John Wheeler, Ed Sikorski.

Middle Row: Rudy Kimiecik, Coach Alex F. Paul, Charles Faliski.

Back Row: Stanley Stopa, Ken Parmerter, William Pillmeier.

The Florida Athletic Club
c. 1905
Photographed by James Razey
Reprinted from Florida Historical book [2]

Back Row: Ted Totten (scorekeeper), Ralph Quackenbush, Dave Suresky (?), Bill Gross, Michael J. Barry (manager), Philip Pines (pitcher,?), John Quackenbush, John Arnott(?); Front row: Leon Ramage, Harry Totten (?), Stub Quackenbush, John Mars (catcher,?), Ray Quackenbush (pitcher).

S. S. Seward Institute Junior Varsity Basketball
c. 1947
Collection of John and Dorothy Kimiecik

Front Row: Daniel Kimiecik, Stanley Volock, Dick Parmerter;
Back Row: George Plock, Casimir Rosinski.

S. S. Seward Inst. Baseball
c. 1945
Collection of John and Dorothy Kimiecik
William Pillmeier, John Kimiecik.

Skiing at Mt. Peter
c. 1930
Collection of Bill Raynor

Ice Boats on Greenwood Lake
c. 1910
Historical Society of the Town of Warwick

Golfing in Warwick
c. 1915
Historical Society of the Town of Warwick, Joslyn Collection

This image shows the golf links in back of the Red Swan Inn. This golf course, which is now part of the Warwick Country Club, is nearly a hundred years old! Railway office and shops can be seen in the background.

The Historical Society of the Town of Warwick

Fun at the Lake
1913
Collection of Beattie, Jacob, and May Family

Beattie family having fun at a the lake. It's not news that swimming has always been a popular summer pastime in Warwick, but swim gear has changed dramatically. Men wore full suits instead of just shorts about ninety years ago, and women covered not only their hair but their legs as well.

Lake Slide
c. 1910
Historical Society of the Town of Warwick, Joslyn Collection

Lakeside playground equipment has not changed all that much in 100 years.

Warwick Gun Club
1902
Historical Society of the Town of Warwick, Joslyn Collection

The Warwick Gun Club members were champion shooters.

Deer Hunting
c. 1915
Historical Society of the Town of Warwick, Joslyn Collection

We do not know who the hunters were, but there apparently was some good deer hunting around the turn of the century.

Notes

1. Date derived from appearance of stereograph mount.
2. *Florida, New York, Orange County : An Early Look at its Faces, Places and Winding Staircases*, by The Florida Historical Society in Florida, New York, © 2002.
3. *Under Old Rooftrees - an Early Portrait*, by Eliza B. Hornby, 1908.
4. Further information about Hathorn can be found in the Warwick Historical Papers, in "Revolution in the Valley: A Compilation of Documents for the Hathorn Family Reunion" by S. Gardner, and on the Warwick Valley History Web site at www.albertwisnerlibrary.org/~wisner/Factsandhistory/History/Main.htm. Letter to Lyman Draper is part of the Draper Manuscript collection owned by the Wisconsin Historical Society.
5. See "James P. Young's House" online at Warwick Valley History: www.albertwisnerlibrary.org/~wisner/Factsandhistory/History/Young.htm. Documents showing that he treated Aaron Burr were with his papers filed at the Orange County Clerk's office when he died; copies are in collection of James Cline.
6. The only book length biography of Henry William Herbert that has been written is *Frank Forester (Henry William Herbert): A Tragedy in Exile*, by William Southworth.
7. This drawing of Ward, signed "Van Ingen" and titled "Tom Draw in His Double-Seated Wagon" appeared in all editions of Herbert's "My Shooting Box," Volume 1 of "Frank Forester's *Complete Book of Sporting Scenes and Characters*." The memorial essay was published starting in the 5th edition (c. 1881) The essay was also reprinted as a pamphlet in 1846 by the Middletown Whig Press. The Historical Society owns a photocopy of the original handwritten document, source unknown. The artist "Van Ingen" may have been Henry Van Ingen (1833-1899), a Dutch-born artist who taught painting at Vassar beginning in the 1860s.
8. For further information see www.newingtoncropsey.org. There are also several books which contain his local paintings at the Albert Wisner Public Library.
9. *History of the Amity Presbyterian Church, Amity, Orange County, New York*, by Carrie Timlow Feagles.
10. This is the original stone bridge in Bellvale. Built in 1832 to take the place of an older wooden one, this one was replaced in the 1930s with a modern steel bridge as part of a road improvement program.
11. Information from back of original photo. Articles about the Wheeler homestead appeared in the *Warwick Valley Dispatch*, 10/14/1925 and 2/9/1927.
12. *History of Warwick, New York: Three Centuries of a Community 1696-1996*, by Richard Hull, ©1996, p. 60.
13. *History of Warwick, New York: Three Centuries of a Community 1696-1996*, by Richard Hull, ©1996, p. 30. Documentary evidence of the story of its use as an inn is confirmed in the diary of Dr. Increase Matthews, *The New England Historical and Genealogical Register*, Vol. LXXXVI, 1932, "A Journey to the Ohio Country, 1798", p. 35. He stopped on July 1, 1798. It is transcribed as "Pasts" instead of "Posts". Memoir of Paul Case was published in a newspaper, probably the *Dispatch* or *Advertiser*, blurred date appears to be 1898. Photocopy of clipping in Albert Wisner Public Library local history files under "Edenville." Jacobus' will was recorded Liber D., p. 479.
14. Information compiled as part of the menu at Country Dream Restaurant.
15. This legend is referred to in "Looking Back" column of *Dispatch*, 2/2/2002, p. 7.
16. From *Greenwood Lake and West Milford News*, 75th Anniversary Issue, Summer 1999, p. 38, article by Steve Gross.
17. See notes on the history of the Steamer in the *Greenwood Lake and West Milford News* 75th Anniversary Edition, Summer 1999, p. 38, article by Steve Gross.
18. Information on history of property and families owning it was taken from: www.dupontcastle.com/castles/ny_unk11.htm.
19. Warwick *Dispatch* Jan. 3, 1934 "Just Another Little Post Office Closed."
20. Information on Beardsly taken from the *Warwick Historical Papers*, p. 214, and also "Early Days in Warwick" by W. B. Sayer, which appeared in the *Dispatch* March 31- May 12 1898. It is transcribed on the Warwick Valley History Web site at www.albertwisnerlibrary.org/~wisner/Factsandhistory/History/Main.htm.

21. See *Old Landmarks About Warwick Town* by Genevieve M. VanDuzer published in the *Dispatch* March 21, 1917. The problem with the dam is also discussed more in-depth in the memoirs of Nathaniel Jones (copies at the Albert Wisner Public Library and the Historical Society of the Town of Warwick).

22. Information taken from photocopy of *Advertiser* article on file as Albert Wisner Public Library (AWPL), unknown date. Further family information at familysearch.org.

23. From *New York Postal History* by John L. Kay and Chester M. Smith, 1982. Information on "Centre School" taken from teacher contract document from the early 1800s auctioned on EBay in 2004; Historical society has a scan of the page. Location is confirmed by School District no. 19 description.

24. *Advertiser*, 7/3/1902 & 1/9/1929 (second reference may be the *Dispatch*).

25. *Warwick Historical Papers* reprint, p. 12-a, 1906. Birth date for Israel Wood from The Church of Jesus Christ of Latter-Day Saints records, www.familysearch.org. Further information in Dispatch 6/6/1917.

26. Information on Cornelius Board comes from www.ringwoodmanor.com/peo/brdodg/brdodg.htm; the reference is taken from the proceedings of the Wawayanda and Cheesecock Patent dispute.

27. More about the Ames Family can be learned from *Forging ahead: The Ames Family of Easton, Massachusetts and Two Centuries of Industrial Enterprise, 1635-1861*, by Gregory J. Galer.

28. Information on Fairbanks scales can be found at www.ironhorse129.com/rollingstock/builders/fairbanks.htm.

29. See memoirs of Nathaniel Jones, typescript in the collection of the Historical Society of the Town of Warwick.

30. *Warwick Historical Papers*, Orange County Genealogical Society edition, p. 68.

31. *Greenwood Lake and West Milford News,* 75th Anniversary Edition, Summer 1999, pgs. 9, 30,31, articles by Stephen Gross.

32. Obituary of Edward B. Lewis, *Warwick Historical Papers* reprint, p. 175. See also history of Borden's, *Dispatch* 7/3/1907.

33. See *Dispatch* 9/21/1916; *Advertiser* 1/6/1916; obituary in *Brooklyn Daily Standard Union*, 1/6/1918, online at: www.bklyn-genealogy-info.com/Newspaper/BSU/1918.1.html.

34. Notice of relocation *Advertiser* 6/20/1901. Notice of sale of building, *Advertiser* 1/16/1902.

35. *Advertiser* 6/20/1901, Fabric fire hose company notice of moving.

36. See *Dispatch* or *Advertiser*, 3/6/1907 and 1/20/1929.

37. From the *History of Forester Square* by Hylah Hasbrouck available at www.albertwisnerlibrary.org/~wisner/Factsandhistory/History/ForesterSquarebyHasbrouck.htm

38. See history of the business published in the *Advertiser* Supplement, Dec. 1907.

39. *Dispatch* 7/02/1947.

40. From *Greenwood Lake and West Milford News*, 75th Anniversary Issue, Summer 1999, p. 9, article by Steve Gross.

41. For more information about the Orange Blossoms, you can read *This Regiment of Heroes: A Compilation of Primary Materials Pertaining to the 124th New York State Volunteers*, by Charles LaRocca or *The History of the 124th New York State Volunteers* by Captain Charles H. Weygant.

42. More information is in the Albert Wisner Library local history files under "Airplanes and Aviation." Articles about the launch appeared in *The New York Times* on Nov. 10, 1935; Feb. 10, 1936, p. 19; Feb. 24, 1936 p.19. There is also an article in *Rocketmail Flights of the World to 1986* by Dr. Max Kronstein (American Air Mail Society, 1986).

43. History of the Church taken from their Web site at: gbgmchurches.gbgm-umc.org/bellvale/new_page_2.htm.

44. See *History of Forester Square* by Hylah Hasbrouck, see www.albertwisnerlibrary.org/~wisner/Factsandhistory/History/ForesterSquarebyHasbrouck.htm.

45. Sawmill statistics from www.usgennet.org/usa/ny/county/orange/, transcription of Baldwin, Thomas and J. Thomas, M.D. *New and Complete Gazetteer of the United States*. Philadelphia, PA: Lippincott, Grambo, & Co., 1854. Also (Williams, Pg 161).

46. See *Times Herald Record*, 1/11/1999.
47. See obituary of J.H. Crissey, *Dispatch* 4/16/1919.
48. *Dispatch* 10/16/1907.
49. Note on pony cart delivery in "Looking back" column of *Dispatch*, May 23, 1956. History of house from *Report on Valley House* by Kimmy Griffin, 1970 (local history files, Albert Wisner Public Library, and in collection of the Historical Society of the Town of Warwick).
50. Terry Hann has recently gathered many articles about the history of New Milford and its school, which are collected as the *Historical Papers of New Milford, NY* in the collection of Albert Wisner Library. The article about the New Milford school's rebuilding appeared in the Dispatch 5/17/1922.
51. Warwick Seminary: Tuition receipt on collection of Historical Society of the Town of Warwick. High school class number: *Headley's History of Orange Co.*, p. 619.
52. The empty school was later used as a canning facility for the public to use, and eventually torn down by Nielsen Construction.
53. A history of the New York City Farm appears in *Alcoholism in America* by Sarah W. Tracy. Articles on the opening and closing of the farm appeared in *The New York Times* 8/25/1912 p. 11 and *Advertiser* 9/05/1918. Reference for Henry Board Wisner from *History of Warwick, New York: Three Centuries of a Community 1696-1996*, by Richard Hull, ©1996, p. 27.
54. For more information on the history of this institution, see Web site http://www.geocities.com/MotorCity/Downs/3548/facility/midorange.html. Copies are also in the local history files, Albert Wisner Library.
55. From *St. Anthony Hospital and the Franciscan Sisters of the Poor* by Rose Margaret Delany, SFP and David Flood, OFM, 2000. Articles on dedication of hospital appeared in *Dispatch* 4/19/1939.
56. *History of Warwick, New York: Three Centuries of a Community 1696-1996*, by Richard Hull, ©1996, p. 56, and also article by Van Duzer in the *Warwick Historical Papers* reprint edition, p. 27.
57. The Wawayanda House stood nearly opposite the intersection of Forester Ave. and Colonial Ave., where a duplex house now stands. The railings on the porch of duplex are from the hotel.
58. *History of Warwick, New York: Three Centuries of a Community 1696-1996*, by Richard Hull, ©1996, p. 60.
59. See note on owners of Germania House, in "Looking Back" (1906) of 5/23/1956 issue of *Dispatch*.
60. *History of Warwick, New York: Three Centuries of a Community 1696-1996*, by Richard Hull, ©1996, p. 58 & 59
61. Railroad Ave. businesses changed over the years, just as they do today. As near as we can guess, the space in front of Demerest Hall (courtyard area at center) was where the store of H. D. House stood.
62. From *Greenwood Lake and West Milford News*, 75th Anniversary Issue, Summer 1999, p. 22, article by Steve Gross.
63. *Dispatch* 9/18/1907; also 10/2/1907.
64. For more information on the Glider Club, see "Aviation" in the local history files of the Albert Wisner Library.
65. Information is from the *Dispatch*, Sept. 5, 1956.
66. Notes from clippings from the *Warwick Dispatch* in the collection of Raymond Hose Co.
67. For more information on Grinnell Burt and the Railroad, see *Lehigh & Hudson River: History and Operations of the L&HR 1860-1976* by JIm Boyd and Tracy Antz.
68. *History of Warwick, New York: Three Centuries of a Community 1696-1996*, by Richard Hull, ©1996, p. 137
69. Information on Barney came from Michael Diffily of Massachusettes. A report on his activities is in the *Advertiser*, 3/2/1916.
70. SFDL Information from *History of Warwick, New York: Three Centuries of a Community 1696-1996*, by Richard Hull, ©1996, p. 137 and *Greenwood Lake and West Milford News*, 75th Anniversary Issue, Summer 1999.

Index

Symbols

124th Regiment 147
1810 House 100

A

A & P Store 137
Accidents 122, 224, 228
Adams, L. D. 134
Advertiser 9
African Americans 58, 145, 197
Ainsworth, Allen 129
Akin's Pharmacy 203
Aladdin 21
Alaska 16
Albert Wisner Library 88, 168, 212
Alcoholism treatment centers 195
Alexander, William 118
American Air Mail Society 152
American Gazetteer 82
Ames family 119
Amity (hamlet) 24
Amity Cornet Band 24
Amity House 25
Amity Presbyterian Church 24, 27
Amusement Parks 64
Anderson, W. T. 96
Appalachian Trail 58
Apples 182
Applewood Winery 105
Apprenticeship 36
Arlington 63
Armstrong 189
Arnold, Frank L. 8
Arnott, John 239
Aske, Benjamin 76, 88, 97, 104
Aspell House 46, 47, 146, 209
Aspell, J., Miss 136
Assembly of God churches 157
Atlantic White Cedar 82
Automobile garages 47
Automobiles 133
Axes 168

B

Baily 236
Baird, Francis 88, 98
Baird, Samuel Denton 110
Baird, William 110
Baird's Lane 110
Baird's Tavern 88, 130
Baldwin Locomotive Works 224
Bands 24, 184, 213
Bandstands 144
Bank St. 142
Banks 88
Baptist churches 158
Baron, Sandy 82
Barr Castle 21
Barry, Michael J. 239
Baseball players 58, 65
Basket making 36
Basketball teams 238
Baskets 167
Bates, Wade 175
Batz Family 33
Batz, Michael 33
Beardsley, Charles, Col. 88, 97
Beattie Family 147, 181, 241
Beattie, John J. 100, 180
Belcher's Creek 21
Bellvale 30, 120, 167, 188
Bellvale and Monroe Turnpike 30
Bellvale Lakes Rd. 68
Bellvale Mountain 59
Bellvale Rising Star 30
Bellvale Store 31, 32
Bender, Charlie 184
Benedict 236
Benedict, James 147
Benedict Mansion 101
Benedict, William 90, 101
Benjamin, James 111
Big Island Rd. 44, 119
Big V 46
Billy Barnes' Turf Exchange 222
Bird houses 220
Birds 210
Black Dirt 82, 172, 176, 177
Black Dirt region 151
Black Rock Road 21
Blacksmith shops 36
Blacksmiths 24
Blizzards 42, 176
Blooms Corners Rd. 41
Borden Company 76, 124-126, 176
Borden Condensery 79, 232
Borden, John G. 124
Border dispute (NY-NJ) 106
Borkowski, Lou 238
Boxers 58
Boyd, James 238
Boyd, Mary Edith Green 55
Boyer, R. L. 20
Bradner, Benjamin 30
Bradner, H. K., Dr. 199
Bradner, John 30
Bradner, Judge 82
Bradner, Morris Renfrew, Dr. 199
Brandon House 210
Brickyards 127
Bridge St. 55
Bridges 30, 32, 55, 78, 114, 116
Brookland 44
Brooklyn 36
Brooks, James 120
Brooks, Joseph 30
Brookside Farm 68
Brown, C., Jr. 15
Buckwheat 173
Building, Professional 48
Burger King 184
Burk, Albert 199, 203
Burr, Aaron 19, 118
Burr, David H. 24
Burroughs, John 180
Burt, Daniel 30, 100, 106
Burt, Grinnell 147, 200, 220, 229
Burt, James 18, 30, 88
Burt, Thomas 30
Burt's Lane 166
Buses 175
Butler, W. F. 207
Buttonwood 9

C

Caldwell, Solomon 58, 155
Calvary Baptist Church 158
Camps 199
Carlin, Gabriel 82
Carr 189
Carriage shops 19
Cary, Fred 142, 144, 179
Casterline, Charles 191
Castle Garden (NYC) 72
Castle Tavern 123
Castles 65
Catholics 155
Cemetery, Edenville 14
Center (hamlet) 108
Chamber of Commerce 88
Chamberlain, James A. 101
Chardevoyne, W. 96
Chateau Hathorn 107, 170
Cheesecock Patent 30, 58
Chicago 116
Children 178, 183, 186, 187
Chocolate Factory 126
Christ Episcopal Church 158
Christansie, Cornelius 76
Christie 100
Christman, Wilbur 58
Christmas Store 136
Christmast 146

Church of The Good Shepherd 154
Church St. (Village of Warwick) 18
Churches 24, 27, 39, 72, 73
City of New York 195
Civil War 16, 76, 147
Clam Bake 149
Clancey, John and Virginia 38, 40-42
Clarence DeKay store 136
Clark 236
Clark and Thompson 76, 122
Clark, Squire 122
Clasons 36
Clawson, Samuel 76
Cline, James 19
Clintonite 24
Clock Tower 160
Cloth factories 76
Clute, Katherine 27
Coaches 207
Coal 221
Coe, Elias Van Arsdale 14
Coleman, Bill 36
Coleman, Merritt 76
Colonial Ave 90-91, 144, 202
Colwell, B. C. 42
Commercials 110
Commuting 175
Conklin and Strong 79, 115
Conklin, Elmire and Howard 119
Conklin, George R. 131
Conklin, Peter 33
Conklin, Webb 167
Conklin(g), Nathaniel E. 49
Continental Congress 195
Convents 161
Cooley, Isaac F. 21
Cooley, Maria 21, 58
Cooper shops 36
Cornet Band 213
Correctional facilities 195
Country Chevy Olds 91
Country Club 240
Country Dream Restaurant 40, 140
Covered Bridge Rd. 110, 122
Cowdrey Family 144
Cowdrey, John 130
Cranes 228
Crawford, C. C. 134
Crawford's Store 134
Creameries 124, 126
Crissey, Charles A. 142
Crissey, Joel Henry 30, 180
Cropsey, Jasper F. 21, 58, 121
Cuddeback, W. 82

D

Dairies 199
Dairy industry 82, 124, 125
Dams 58
Daniel Sayer 107
Dator, John 98
Daubert 72
Daubert, John 73
Daughters of the American Revolution (DAR) 118
Dayton & Tannery's Orchestra 24
Dead man (traffic sign) 40
Decker 236
Declaration of Independence 195
Deer hunting 242
DeKay, Clarence 136
DeKay, Clarence and Elizabeth 51
DeKay, Don 51, 238
Dekay, Robert 76
DeKay, Thomas 76
Demarest & Lazear 76
Demarest, Jacobus 105
Demarest, Rensallaer 142
Demerest House 205, 213, 222
Demerest, Thomas 204
Depression 58
Dietrich, Ernest G. W. 107, 206
Dill House 47, 209
Dill, Justus 19, 47, 163
Dill, William 47
Diseases 82, 97, 199
Doc Fry Community Center 194
Doctors 14, 19, 22, 24, 44, 50, 51, 52, 132
Dolson 97
Doublekill 76, 79
Drew, A. H. 137
Drowned Lands 24, 72, 82
Drunkard's Rock 59
Dubois 100
Dunning, Benjamin F. 183
Durland 195
Dusinberre, Daniel Coe 14
Dutch 58, 105
Dutch Hollow 58, 108

E

Eager, Samuel W. 44
Edal, Jim 184
Edenite 24
Edenville 14, 140, 171, 184
Edenville Hotel 39
Edenville Inn 184
Edenville Methodist Church 39
Edenville Rd. 19, 38
Edenville Store 140
Edsall, Clara 147
Edsall, R. L. 96
Edward J. Lempka Dr. 54
Edwards, H. R. 40
Ehlers, Chick 238
Electricity 44, 97
Ellis Island 72
Elm St. Yard 224
Elston, Roy 126
Embler, Mary Boyd 55
England 20
Erie Railroad 82, 232, 233
Erskine 24
Eurich 72
Everett, G. S. 42
Everett, George S. 40
Everett, Seely 40, 42, 140
Excelsior Hose 216

F

Fabric Fire Hose Company 128, 215
Factories 128, 129
Factory St. 128
Falck, Willie 214
Faliski, Charles 238
Farries, A. P., Dr. 132
Feagles, Carrie Timlow 24
Felczak, John S., Msgr. 84, 85, 151, 172, 177
Feldner, Marty 68
Ferrier, Thomas 24
Ferris Wheels 64
Fire companies 98, 128, 215, 216, 217
Fire departments 44
Fire hose 128
Fires 76, 96, 101, 204
First National Bank 142
First National Bank of Warwick 88
First Presbyterian Church 44
First St. 157
Fish, John and Mary 50
Fishing 132, 178, 180
Floods 82, 177, 228
Florida 16, 19, 22, 44, 111, 119, 127, 132, 146, 162, 163, 189, 190, 191, 217, 232, 238
Florida Auto Company 133
Florida Historical Society 46, 47, 52, 127
Florida Lyceum 191
Florida Union Free School District 16
Flowers 167
Foght, John Morris 158
Folklore and oral tradition 65, 189

Food preservation 182
Forester Ave. 100, 149, 158, 202, 221
Forester, Frank 20, 58, 82, 202
Forester Square 144, 147, 212
Forges 30
Forshee's Garage 99, 133
Four Corners Rd. 105, 187
Fourth of July 47
Franciscan Sisters of the Poor 101
Frank Forester monument 212
Franklin Marble 24
Fraternal organizations 213
Freeman, Ira 197
French, Daniel Chester 16
Fulling (textiles) 120
Funerals 73

G

Gale, S. E. 82
Galloway Rd. 158, 166, 207
Gardening 168
Gardner, Samuel F. 111
Garfield, President 109
Garvilla, Ignatius 238
Geology 19, 24
Gerlitz 72, 74
German-Russian 172
Germania House 203
Germans 72
Germany 126, 152
Gettysburg 147
Gifford, Nancy 15
Gillespie, James 128
Gilvan's (store) 174
Glenmere 184
Glenmere Ave. 52, 162
Glenmere Lake 54
Glider Club 214
Gobel, Sam 36
Golet 184
Golf 240
Goodwill Hook and Ladder 98, 215
Gorish, Farries 47
Goshen 147
Governor of New York 16
Grand Army of the Republic 147
Granges 115
Great Dane Trucking 121
Great Depression 58
Green Blacksmith & Carriage Shop 55
Green, Henry 36, 55
Green, Samuel 217
Greenhouses 183
Greenwood Forest Farms 58
Greenwood Lake 21, 58, 59, 152, 154, 155, 210, 233
Greenwood Lake and Montclair Railroad 233
Greenwood Lake Association 210
Greenwood Lake Public Beach 64
Greenwood Lake Transportation Co. 63
Greenwood Lake Village 58
Greenwoods Rd. 108
Gridley, John C. 135
Grinding wheels 168
Grinnell Burt 220
Grist mills 119
Gross, Bill 239
Gross, Steven 58
Gudewill, H.E. 65
Guns 242

H

Haaren, Conrad 126
Hair 181
Halfway House 36
Handcars 69, 231
Handcrafts 167
Hann, Casper and Terry 76, 120, 122
Hardware stores 134
Harrison, Thomas 76
Harvests 37
Hasbrouck , Hylah 18
Hasbrouck, Lydia Sayer 107
Hasenclever, Peter 58
Hathorn House 106, 107
Hathorn, John 15, 24, 76, 104, 106, 118
Hathorn Park 194
Hathorn Road 15
Hay 33
Hay harvesting 170, 171
Haymakers (fraternal organization) 213
Hebrew Community Center 164
Hemmer, Peter 108
Henderson 39-40
Herbert, Henry William 20, 58, 82, 202
Heron, James, Dr. 19
Hewitt 152
High School 194
High St. 192, 215
Highland Ave. 53
Highland Engine and Hose Co. No. 3 217
Historic Sites 65, 98, 108
Historical markers 118
Historical Society of Middletown 107
Holy Rosary R. C. Church 155
Hoodoo Parade 144
Horse auctions 146
Horses 76
Horton, J. M. 124
Horton, Martin Van Buren 175, 224
Hotels and Inns 25, 39, 98, 202, 232
House, H. D. 139
Houseboats 64
Houston 189
Houston Farm (Edenville) 41
Houston, Henry W. 14
Houston, J. Wood, Capt. 147
Houston, James W. 40
Houston, Joseph 36, 171
Houston, Phebe 14
Houston, S. 52
Howe St. 128
Howell, William and Audrey 49, 134
Howell's Meadow View Farm 54
Hoyt 130, 199
Hoyt Rd. 199
Hudson River School 21
Hughes, Langston 58
Hull Family 105
Hull, Richard 63, 88, 126
Hunting 242
Hyatt, G. W. 226
Hylah Hasbrouck 147
Hynard Brothers 222
Hynard, Wm. 130

I

Ice cream 124, 140
Ice industry 174, 176
Immigrants 44, 72, 82, 126, 162, 170, 172, 174
Improved Order of the Red Men 213
Inns and hotels 37, 41, 76, 82, 190
Interiors 140, 141, 157, 179
Inventions 128
Iron Act 30
Iron industry 30, 58, 119
Iron Mountain Rd. 119
Iroquois 60

J

J.M. Horton Ice Cream Co. 124
Jackson, Joe 58
Jagodnaja Poljana 72
Jansen, Jan and Elizabeth 53
Jardine, Mr. 157
Jayne, Bill 217
Jayne, Dewitt Clinton, Dr. 50
Jayne St. 232
Jennings, Mary 48
Jessup 189

Jeter, Derek 65
Jockey Hollow 36, 76
Johnson, Andrew 16, 44
Johnson, Solomon W. 101
Jones, Mary Burt 18
Jones, Nathaniel 18, 30, 192
Joslyn Collection 33
Joslyn, Duane 9
Judges 180
June, Theodore H. 213

K

Keiran, John 76
Keene Publishing 2
Kennedy, John 209
Kennedy Tavern 44
Kessler, Fred W. 152
Ketchum, Azariah 158
Ketchum, Florence 151
Ketchum, Samuel 33
Key Bank 130
Kiel 72
Kimiecik, John and Dorothy 45, 49, 133, 136
Kimiecik, Rudy 238
Kings Highway 68, 104, 126, 202
Kleveno 72
Knapp, Charles 24
Knapp, J. W. 85
Knife Factory 129
Knives 128
Knolls 101
Kohler, Louis 210

L

L.D. Adams Hardware Store 134
Ladders 181
Lake (hamlet) 68, 126
Lake St. 166
Lake Station 69
Lake Station Rd. 68, 126, 188
Lamplighters 93, 134
Landmarks 59, 108
Langlitz 24, 72, 74
Lawrence 236
Lawrence, Thomas 214
Lawrence, Virginia 214
Lawton (hamlet) 68
Layton, Lewis 24
Lazear, Cornelius 131, 160
Lazear, John 76
Legends & oral tradition 59
Lehigh and Hudson River Railway 88, 116
Leinweber 72
Lenape 58, 60, 90, 106

Lenapes 104
Lewis, Charles W. 144
Lewis, Edward B. 124
Lewis, Madison 101, 158
Lewis Park 215
Ley, Willy 152
Libraries 212
Limerock Island 154
Lincoln, Abraham 16, 44, 50
Linden Pl. 90
Litchfield, Dominy 147
Little York 187
Little York Rd. 73, 74
Lomax, Don and Kathryn 41
Long Pond 58
Longhouse Creek 30, 32, 120
Longwell, John 236
Lorillard estate 53
Louis, Joe 58
Lower Wisner Rd 30
Lucha, John 214
Luchi 236
Lucznikowska, Valerie 25, 26, 130
Luft 72
Lumber 169
Lust 72
Lutheran churches 72
Lutheran Parochial School 74

M

Mabee 53
Mabee, Ethel 178
Mabel Boyd 55
Macy's (store) 199
Main St. (Amity) 25
Main St. (Bellvale) 31
Main St. (Florida) 16, 45, 46, 50, 133, 134, 135, 136, 146, 163, 189, 209, 217
Main St. (Greenwood Lake) 61
Main St. (Warwick Village) 9
Main St. (Warwick) 88, 91, 95, 99, 130, 137, 140, 144, 145, 160, 179, 202, 203, 213, 215, 229
Malaria 82
Mann, W.M. 30
Mansions 101
Mapes, Mortimer 48
Maple Ave. 101, 180, 183
Maple Ave. (Florida) 125, 132, 232
Mars, Jesse D., Dr. 51, 52
Mars, John 239
Masonic building 92
Masonic lodges 213
Mastodons 82

Matthews, Susie 46
Mauge, Conrad E., Jr. 197
McConnell, John 14, 24
McConnell, Milton 14
McConnell, Norman 24
McDaniels, George 82
McElroy, Henry 157
McEwen St. 140, 203
McEwen, Thomas 18
McGuffie 27
McKee, John 18
McPeek, Harvey 159
McPherson, Mary Bahrman 76
Meadow Rd. 127
Memorial Park 147
Methodist Church 51, 140
Methodist Episcopal Church 160, 163
Mexico 172
Mid State Correctional Facility. 195
Migrant workers 172
Military Service 72
Milk boxcars 223
Mill in the Glen 44
Mill Pond 31
Miller 72, 236
Miller, G.A. 96
Miller, Hazel 40, 140
Miller's Creek 55
Millinary shops 135
Mills 30, 32, 44, 76, 79, 109, 114, 119, 120, 121, 122, 169
Mining 36
Minisink and Warwick Turnpike 76
Minsi 58
Minsi tribe 60, 104
Minturn's General Store 61
Mission of the Immaculate Virgin 82
Mistucky 90, 106
Mistucky Water Celebration 173
Moe (hamlet, NJ) 119
Moe Mtn. 21, 178
Mohr 72
Montclair and Greenwood Lake Railway 58
Montclair. 63
Montgomery Hale Vernon Brickyard 127
Mooney, Edward L. 21
Moonlight scenes 78
Morely, J. F. 8
Morgiewicz, Barbara 25, 62, 83, 84, 85, 151, 172
Morningside County Club 152
Morris 236
Morris Canal and Banking Company 58

Motor Bus Society 175, 176, 177, 210, 223, 227
Mountain Ice House 123
Movies 184
Mt. Adam Granite Company 36, 40
Mt. Alverno 161
Mt. Eve 50
Mt. Eve School 190
Mt. Peter 33, 214
Mt. Peter House 230
Mts. Adam and Eve 37
Muetschele 45, 133
Munsee 58
Murray, Lucy 46
Museum of the American Indian 60
Museum Village 135
Museums 98, 100
Music 24
Musical groups 184, 213
Myruski, Clarence 238

N

Nanny 41
Nanny Family 184
Nanny, Harrison W. 49
Nash, Leonard 238
National Register of Historic Places 16, 65, 92, 106
Native Americans 24, 60, 82, 90, 108, 208
Naturalists 180, 210
New Milford 76, 122, 186, 222
New Milford Methodist Church 160
New Milford School 186
New York State Training School for Boys 195, 198
New York Telephone Company 199
Newhard's 174
Newspapers 9, 88, 96
Night Blooming Cereus 183
Noble family 118
Nowak, Stanislaus J. 161-163

O

Oakland Ave. 101, 166, 184, 203, 231
Oakland Theater 184
Ochs 72
Old School Baptist Meeting House 149, 158
Onion Harvest Festival 45, 150, 151
Onion industry 172, 177
Onions 83
Opera houses 136
Operators (telephone) 141, 199

Orange Blossoms (Civil War) 147
Orange County Medical Society 22
Orchards 181
Ostrom 68
Otness Collection 99
Ott 72
Our Lady of the Lake 155
Out of the Burning 197
Oxen 36, 119, 170

P

Pacem in Terris 122
Packer, Charles E. 191
Paffenroth, Henry 74
Parades 144, 145
Park Ave. 194
Park Avenue School 194
Parks 64, 231
Parmerte, Ken 238
Parochial schools 74, 187
Patent, Wawayanda 88
Paul, Alex F. 238
Peck 30
Pelton Rd. 166
Perna, Frank 184
Perry's Pond 195
Pest control 220
Pets 178
Pfaffenroth 72
Pharmacies 45, 135
Piasecki Family 129
Piekarnia 45
Pierson 189
Pillmeier, William 238
Pine Island 82, 83, 129, 151, 176, 177, 178
Pine Island Branch 232
Pine Island Creamery. 176
Pine Island School 186, 188
Pine Island Tpk 171
Pine Island Tpk. 37, 39, 42
Pinecrest 183
Pines, Philip 239
Pitts, G. F. 101
Plock, Charles 238
Plock, Martha 151
Pobotschnaja 72
Pochuck 24
Pochuck Creek 24
Polish 44, 82, 161, 162, 172
Politicians 16, 18, 37, 44
Poloniak, Louis 129
Pont, Addie 128
Pony carts 183
Post 36
Post, Garrit 100

Post, Jacobus 36, 37
Post offices 18, 32, 46, 76, 82, 152
Postville 36, 37
Potatoes 174
Presbyterian Church 162, 163
Public works 44
Pulaski Highway 83, 85, 124
Purling Brook 36
Purple martins 220

Q

Quackenbush 31
Quackenbush, E. A. 238
Quackenbush, John 239
Quackenbush, Ralph 239
Quackenbush, Ray 239
Quackenbush, Stub 239
Quaker Creek 55
Quampium 58, 60

R

R. H. Macy Co. 199
Racetracks 226
Radio stations 184
Ragone, Doris 61
Railroad 100
Railroad Ave. 139, 174, 204, 205, 220, 222, 225
Railroad Ave. (Florida) 125
Railroad Green 97, 231
Railroad Hotel 222, 232
Railroad stations 69, 79, 100, 116, 220, 226, 233
Railroads 36, 58, 82, 116, 122, 177, 220, 240
Raith, Rev. 162
Ramage, Leon 239
Randall, Gary and Kathy 99
Randall St. 121, 189
Randallville 121
Randallville Mill 44
Randolph Hotel 190
Raymond Hose 128, 215
Raynor, Bill 140, 184
Raynor, Fred Cary 138, 140
Raynor, Lucy Smith 187
Ray's Exxon Service Center 129
Razey, James 9, 180, 217
Red Swan Inn 166, 206, 208, 240
Reform schools 195
Reformed Church 98, 159
Regelski, Adam 238
Religious Orders 91, 101, 161
Revolutionary War 15, 24, 33, 41, 44, 104, 106, 118
Reynolds, Edmund 130

Richard Hull 130
Ridge School 187
Ringwood Co. 123
Roads 30, 36, 59, 76, 169, 202
Robinson, Brower 30
Robinson, Ray (Sugar) 58
Robinson, Victor 19, 31
Rock shelter 60
Rocket Airplane Corporation of America 152
Rocket mail 138, 152
Roe Brothers Inc. 132
Roe, Elizabeth 50
Roe, J. K. 217
Roe, Wheeler 39
Roe, William J. 54
Roecker, E. 31, 32, 33
Roe's Woods 189
Roman Catholic Church 155, 157, 163
Roome, William 58
Roosevelt, Eleanor 151, 196, 197
Rosenberg, William 46
Rosinski, Casimir 239
Roundhouses 227
Rowlee, Heman 36, 41
Rt. 1 39, 108, 166, 171
Rt. 17A 30, 33, 59, 158, 166
Rudy 72, 184
Ruhl 72-73
Russia 72, 170
Ruth, Babe 58
Ryerson, Ed 203
Ryerson, George 58

S

S.S. Seward Institute 16, 22, 44, 48, 190, 191, 238, 239
Sakofsky, Harold 238
Sanford, George W. 91
Sanford, Ezra 15, 109
Sanford Insurance Agency 98
Sanford, John W., Jr. 214
Sanford Memorial Fountain 144, 212
Sanford, Pierson Ezra 106
Sanfordville 36
Sanitoriums 199
Sawmills 119, 169, 175, 224
Sayer, Anna 74
Sayer, Daniel 107
Sayer, Horace G. 24
Sayer, William Benjamin 98, 202
Sayer, William H. 130
Sayerville 107
Sayre, Joseph 142
Sayre, Seely 24
Schadt 72

Schaible, G. C. 238
Scheuermann, Emilie 73, 74
Scheuermann, John, 72
Scheuermann, Harry 73
Schlagel 72
Schloicka, Robert and Robyn 53
Schmick 72, 74
School Dist. No. 3 190
School Dist. No. 4 189
School No. 15 189
School No. 2 189
School on the Rock 189
Schools 27, 74, 76, 186
Schultz, Charles E. 53
Schultz, Joachim Ontario 53
Scott, Bob and Nancy 49
Scrauley, Lawrence 30
Sears Roebuck houses 52
Searsmobile 175
Seely, Richard 214
Seely, Sylvanus 24
Seely, W. S. 85
Servin 147, 199
Seward House, Auburn 48
Seward Institute 107
Seward Monument 16
Seward, Samuel S. 48
Seward, Samuel Sweezy 16, 22, 44, 191
Seward, William Henry 16, 44, 48, 189
Sharps, Edward 62
Sharps, Martha 62
Shawcross, Viner 167
Sherwood Hall 199
Shingle House 37, 100
Shingle House (Edenville) 36
Shoemakers 36
Shooting 242
Shore Ave. 65
Shuback, Ray and Helen 129
Shulman, Isaac 170, 174
Shulman, Max 174
Signalmen 231
Sikorski, Ed 238
Silva Glen 44
Simms Family 25, 68, 69
Sircable 72
Slavery 16
Sleigh, Gloria 152
Sleigh, John 138, 152
Sleighs 36, 173
Slides 241
Sloan, James 76
Sloat Family 53
Sly 189
Smith, Joseph 203

Smith, Lucy 187
Snow 176
Soda Fountain 140
Sodrick, Frances 82
Sodrick, Frances and Bob 178
South St. 98, 100, 157, 174, 177, 228
Spanktown 44
Spanktown Rd. 111, 119, 189
Spanktown Schoolhouse 189
Sprague, Clifton 134
Spring St. 126, 129
St. Anthony Hospital 100-101, 200
St. Edward Roman Catholic Church 44, 163
St. Joseph Roman Catholic Church 44, 162, 163
St. Peter's Evangelical Lutheran Church 72-74
St. Stephen's R. C. Church 44, 155, 157
Staats, Samuel G. 105
Stanaback, J. B. 76
State School Rd 30
Steamers 58, 63
Steen, Nina 61, 62, 63, 65
Sterling Forest 155
Sterling Forest State Park 58, 104, 118
Sterling Forest Station 63
Sterling iron works 104
Sterling Lake 118
Stevens, John Wright 42
Stidworthy, Earl 214
Still 236
Still, Edwin F. 8
Stirling 118
Stoll, Charles 238
Stony Creek 111
Stopa, Stanley 238
Stores 18, 24, 25, 31, 46, 61, 68, 77, 79, 96, 115, 129, 137
Storms 176, 177
Storms, Maude 60
Straton, Suzanne 49
Straub, New 72
Streams 78, 79, 114
Street lamps 134
Strong, George H. 131
Substance abuse programs 195
Sugar Loaf 104
Sunset Inn 101
Sunshine Society 217
Suresky, Dave 239
Swamps 82
Swimming 241
Synagogue 164

T

Tallman, M. B. 45, 135
Tanneries 76
Tate, Florence 32
Taylor, Elihu B. 90
Teachman 58
Teenagers 236
Telephone companies 217
Telephones 141
Television 110
Temple Beth Shalom 164
Ten Eyck, M. F. 203
Ten Railroad Ave. 222
Theaters 136, 184, 191
Thomas, William C. 32
Thompson, Charles 122
Thompson, William 44
Threshing 173
Thunderbird Electronics Mfg. 129
Tiedemann, John 65
Toll gates 33
Tom Draw 20
Tompkins, J. 42
Totten, Harry 239
Totten, Ted 239
Tourism 58
Town Hall 229
Townsend, Peter 118
Toy Chest store 96, 229
Track teams 238
Traffic signals 213
Train wrecks 224, 228
Trusdell 24, 25, 26, 141
Tuberculosis 199
Tuxedo Park 53
Tuxedo Tribe of the Red Men 213

U

Under Old Rooftrees (book) 14
Underground Railroad 82, 111
Union Corners Rd. 37, 38, 40, 171, 189
United States Hotel 144

V

Vail 52
Vail, George S. 51
Vail, Willet 136
Vail, William J. 132
Vail, William L. 45
Van Buren St. 224
Van Duzer, W. W. 90
Van Ingen, Henry 20
Van Ness 203
Van Sickle, Jess and Pauline 178
Vandenburg 46
Vanderburgh, Garfield 134
Vandervort, C. 54
VanDuzer Pl. 180
VanGelder, John 178
VanLeer, Elizabeth Sanford 98
VanNess 183
Vaudeville 58
Vernon, Charles 135
Vernon, Montgomery Hale 51, 127
Vernon's Apothecary 45, 135
Vernon's Brickyard 50
Veterans 147, 148
Victory Supermarket 46
Village Hall 159, 215
Villages (incorporation dates) 104
Villamil, Felix 49, 180
Volga Germans 72
Volock, Stanley 239

W

Wagner 72
Wagon making 36
Wallkill River 82, 177
Ward, General 147
Ward, Thomas 202
Warkill Valley Milk Products Company 126
Warwick Advertiser 9, 88, 96, 97
Warwick Assembly of God 157
Warwick Auto Co. 222
Warwick Conference Center 21, 199
Warwick Glider Club 214
Warwick Grange 115
Warwick Gun Club 242
Warwick High School 236, 237
Warwick Institute 192, 193, 194, 202
Warwick Knife Company 128
Warwick Municipal Airport 214
Warwick Savings Bank 88
Warwick Stage Line 175
Warwick Turnpike 21
Warwick United Methodist Church 160
Warwick Valley Central School District 186
Warwick Valley Dispatch 88
Warwick Valley House 97, 203, 222
Warwick Valley Light and Power Company 225
Warwick Valley Railroad 88, 104, 203, 220
Warwick Valley Telephone Co. 141
Warwick Woodlands 20, 202
Warwickite 24
Washing clothes 69
Washington, George 36, 37, 98, 202
Washington, George Seward 50, 53
Waterbury, Almeda 41
Waterbury, James 41
Waterbury Rd. 36, 41, 184
Waterstone Cottage 154
Waterstone Rd. 61
Waterstone, Satella Sharps 154
Waterstone St. 138
Wawayanda Creek 76, 78, 114, 166, 177, 193
Wawayanda Furnace 119
Wawayanda Hotel 147, 192
Wawayanda House 20, 168, 202
Wawayanda Lake 168
Wawayanda Patent 76
Wawyanda and Cheesecook Patents 118
Waywayanda 30
Weaving 167
Weddings 178
Weed, Irving 238
Weed, John 163
Weeden 236
Weed's Hall 163
Weitz 72
Welles, Frank J. 8, 58, 60
Welling Ave. 194
Welling, Elizabeth 106
Welling, Samuel 90
Welling, Thomas 106
West Milford 21
West Shore 210
West St. 88, 108, 131, 158, 213
WGNY 184
Wheeler 91, 109, 182, 189
Wheeler, Charles W. 182
Wheeler, Joel 33, 179
Wheeler, John 130, 238
Wheeler Rd. 111
Wheeler, Zebulon 44, 119
White, Lurana 91
White, Walter 152
Wickersham, II, Rev. 158
Wickham Lake 195
Wilcox, William 82
Wilcox, William 210
Wilder, Don 170, 180
Wilder, Victor Audubon 107, 170
Wilhelm 72
Wilkins, Paul 184
Willet Vail Opera House 136
Williams, Charles 41
Wilson Bulletin 210
Wilson, Charles 76
Windermere 138
Windermere Ave. 61
Windermere Landing 62

Windermere Recreation Park 64
Windmills 51
Winter 146
Wisner (hamlet) 114, 126
Wisner, Albert 116, 212
Wisner brothers 207
Wisner, Clinton Wheeler 90, 206
Wisner Family 116
Wisner, Henry Board 195
Wisner, James Amherst 183
Wisner, John, Capt. 195
Wisner Rd. 114, 115, 116
Wisner, Roy G. 238
Wisniewski, John 238
Witches 189
Women 199
Women's suffrage 107
Wood 82
Wood, Fred 142
Wood, Israel 114
Wood, Lewis 76
Woodruff, Mattie 46
Woolsey, Charles H. 82
Workmen 169
World War I 148
World War II 152
WPA (Works Progress Administration) 59
Wright, Orville 214
Wyndhurst. 101

Y

Yesterday's restaurant 137
Young, James P. 19, 36
Young, Stewart 50
Youngman, August 72
Youngman, Estella 27
Yungman, Susan M. 72

Historical Society of the Town of Warwick

Mission Statement

The Historical Society of the Town of Warwick believes that an understanding and appreciation of our historic heritage is essential to maintaining a unique and meaningful identity as a community. The mission of the Society is to celebrate and preserve the history of the Town of Warwick and its people and to assure that this legacy is passed on to future generations. Towards this end we will: educate and engage a diverse public through a variety of programs; maintain our museum buildings, properties, and collections; research and publish historic records; identify and encourage preservation of significant places and structures throughout the town; and manage the society openly, ethically, and professionally.

Join us!

The Historical Society of the Town of Warwick was founded in 1906 to preserve, commemorate, and educate the public about the rich heritage of our town.

We own the Old School Baptist Church, the Shingle House, Baird's Tavern, the 1810 House, the Ketchum House, the Sly Barn, the Hasbrouck Carriage House, and the Lehigh and Hudson River Caboose, all in the Village of Warwick. These museum buildings are open during the summer and for special events.

We also own and maintain Lewis Park and the Old School Baptist Cemetery.

We welcome all who are interested to join us in preserving our heritage and educating the public about the rich history of our Town.

To learn more about us, our fundraisers and educational events, and to join, visit our Web site at www.warwickhistoricalsociety.org or call 845-986-3236 and request a membership form.

Historical Society of the Town of Warwick
P. O. Box 353
Warwick, NY 10990
(845) 986-3236

Share Your Warwick Memories…

Help our archive record today's memories for tomorrow.

If these photos remind you of stories, or details about our community you'd like to pass on, jot them down now and send to us! Use the form below, or email to us at info@warwickhistoricalsociety.org.

Name: _____

Street: _____

Town/State/Zip: _____

Phone number: _____   Email: _____

Your memories:

_____
_____
_____
_____
_____
_____
_____
_____
_____

Historical Society of the Town of Warwick
P. O. Box 353
Warwick, NY 10990
(845) 986-3236

Quick Order Form

(40% Donation goes to Warwick Historical Society)

- Fax this form to: 845-987-7845
- Telephone: 845-987-7750 **(have your credit card ready)**
- Email orders: info@KeeneBooks.com
  (or order online at www.KeeneBooks.com)
- Postal Orders: Keene Publishing PO Box 54 Warwick, NY 10990

☐ **YES**, please send me the following copies of ***Days Gone By: A History in Pictures Town of Warwick, New York***

QTY	PRICE	TOTAL
_____ X	$29.00 =	_____
Shipping & Handling*		_____
Sales Tax**		_____
Total Amount Due		_____

* Shipping costs: Ground — $ 4 first book, $1 each addl.
                   Express — $12 first book, $2 each addl.
  Bulk orders: call for best shipping rates and qty. discount.
**Please add on sales tax for books shipped to NY or PA.

Payment

☐ Check   ☐ Visa   ☐ Mastercard   ☐ Amex   ☐ Discover

Please make checks payable to **Keene Publishing**

Card Number: _____   Exp. Date: ___/___

3-digit Verification # on back of card: _____

Phone or email, in case of problem: _____

Name (print): _____   Signature: _____

Organization: _____

Billing Address: _____

City: _____   State: _____   Zip: _____

Note: If you would like to have books shipped to a different address than your billing address, please provide that address on a separate page.

Thank you for your order!

**Would your town's historical society like to raise funds by doing a history in pictures such as this book?
If so, contact the publisher, Diane Tinney, at 845-987-7750.**